Literature in Perspective

General Editor: Kenneth H. Grose

The Elizabethan Poets

Literature in Perspective

The Elizabethan Poets

The Making of English Poetry from Wyatt to Ben Jonson

Fred Inglis

Evans Brothers Limited, London

Published by Evans Brothers Limited
Montague House, Russell Square, London, W.C.1

© Fred Inglis 1969

First published 1969

To my Father and Mother

Set in 11 on 12 point Bembo and printed in Great Britain
by The Camelot Press Ltd., London and Southampton
237 35100 5 cased   PR 1444
237 35101 3 limp

Literature in Perspective

Reading is a pleasure; reading great literature is a great pleasure, which can be enhanced by increased understanding, both of the actual words on the page and of the background to those words, supplied by a study of the author's life and circumstances. Criticism should try to foster understanding in both aspects.

Unfortunately for the intelligent layman and young reader alike, recent years have seen critics of literature (particularly academic ones) exploring slender ramifications of meaning, exposing successive levels of association and reference, and multiplying the types of ambiguity unto seventy times seven.

But a poet is 'a man speaking to men', and the critic should direct his efforts to explaining not only what the poet says, but also what sort of man the poet is. It is our belief that it is impossible to do the first without doing the second.

LITERATURE IN PERSPECTIVE, therefore, aims at giving a straightforward account of literature and of writers—straightforward both in content and in language. Critical jargon is as far as possible avoided; any terms that must be used are explained simply; and the constant preoccupation of the authors of the Series is to be lucid.

It is our hope that each book will be easily understood, that it will adequately describe its subject without pretentiousness so that the intelligent reader who wants to know about Donne or Keats or Shakespeare will find enough in it to bring him up to date on critical estimates.

Even those who are well read, we believe, can benefit from a lucid expression of what they may have taken for granted, and perhaps—dare it be said?—not fully understood.

K. H. G.

The Elizabethan Poets

This book has two aims. The first is to describe an intellectual and historical context and to bed certain poets within that context. The poets in question are important but most of them are commonly neglected. Consequently, in describing and attempting to judge these poets, I am further attempting in a modest way to adjust a little the particular groups of poets honoured and read today, and the standards by which we choose them. Although there is a tremendously large number of books upon Elizabethan poetry there is none, so far as I know, which takes the poets I take with the same exclusiveness, or treats them in the same way. But I would not wish to press any claims to idiosyncratic originality. The Elizabethans perfected the short poem in English. The work they did holds through for four hundred years. Amongst the host of moderate material and of rubbish, I have chosen those poets who seem to me to have permanent and serious claims upon our attention; I have chosen them not because they are 'relevant', but because they are good.

In moving towards these views I have been helped by a variety of reading, and I list these critical helps, as well as the editions I have used, chapter by chapter in the bibliography. Since this is not a volume concerned with textual problems, I have modernised for myself all the texts which I quote. But there are one or two tributes I am eager to pay here. The first is to that most distinguished critic Yvor Winters, whose writing about Elizabethan poets has decisively altered my reading of them. The second is to Dr. John Williams, whose anthology *English Renaissance Poetry* (Doubleday 1963) is first and best in the field, regrettably hard to purchase in this country, and who sponsored my own anthology *English Poetry 1550–1660* (Methuen 1965); I am glad to thank him for his teaching and his guidance. Last and most importantly, I am proud to thank for his friendship, editorial incisiveness and inexhaustible humour, Kenneth Grose.

And then my wife who did all the typing.   F. C. I.

Contents

The Author

Fred Inglis, M.A., M.Phil., is Senior Lecturer in English at
Southampton College of Education, and author of *Keats* in
this series, and *An Essential Discipline* (Methuen 1968).

7

Acknowledgements

The author and publishers are indebted to Faber and Faber Ltd., London, for permission to reprint the poem 'The House Was Quiet and the World Was Calm' from *Collected Poems* by Wallace Stevens; and to Alfred A. Knopf, Inc., for permission to reprint the same poem from *The Collected Poems of Wallace Stevens*, copyright, 1942, 1947 by Wallace Stevens. The extracts of songs from *An Elizabethan Song Book*, edited by W. H. Auden, Chester Kallman and Noah Greenberg are reprinted by permission of Faber and Faber Ltd., London, and Doubleday & Company Inc., copyright © 1955 by W. H. Auden and Noah Greenberg.

The portrait of Greville (top left) on the cover is reproduced by kind permission of the Ashmolean Museum, Oxford; the portraits of Sidney, Jonson and Wyatt on the cover are reproduced by kind permission of the National Portrait Gallery. The photographs of the rose window, and the screen at Worksop Manor are reproduced by kind permission of the R.I.B.A. Drawings Collection. Every effort has been made to trace owners of the copyright of the photographs of Longleat House and Wollaton Hall, but the publishers wish to apologise to any whose rights may have been unwittingly infringed.

The author also wishes to acknowledge Dr. Andor Gomme for his taste, promptness and scholarship in the selection of illustrations.

I

The Elizabethan Moment

Elizabethan poetry includes some of the greatest poems in our language. But during the upheaval in literary studies which took place sometime between 1912 and 1939 or so, we learned only to look at a certain kind of Elizabethan poetry, and to disregard the rest. The teachers who saw the greatness of men like Donne, Herbert and Marvell effected a revolution, and a thrilling one. When Donne's voice burst with unfamiliar suddenness on 20th-century ears, it was a vivid moment:

> I wonder, by my troth, what thou and I
> Did, till we lov'd? were we not wean'd till then?
> But suck'd on country pleasures, childishly?
> Or snorted we in the Seven Sleepers den?
> 'Twas so . . .
>
> THE GOOD-MORROW

The impatience, the brusque passion, the amazing energy of language, the covert, shocking indecency, the abrupt, stopping movement, all these come as a bright vision to those who have known poetry only in the pale tints of *The Golden Treasury*, or the gentilities of the Georgians. An enthusiasm for Donne and Marvell confirmed and sharpened the finest readers in their amazed acclaim for the new poetry of T. S. Eliot and Ezra Pound. In all the upheaval, the poetry of the Victorians came in for heavy censure, and their taste for the milder Elizabethan sonneteers along with it. In fact, the few songs and sonnets which appear in *The Golden Treasury* and in the earlier editions of the *Oxford Book of English Verse* were taken to *be* Elizabethan poetry,

9

and so a whole tradition largely goes unread, a cluster of other poems goes misunderstood, and a handful of heretical fictions becomes the doctrine of the next generation of students. The poetry which goes unread is the subject of this book; until we read and value that poetry, we shall misread and overvalue the poetry of Donne and the metaphysicals, and worse, we may become partial and tendentious in our reading of the rest of English poetry. It is a bold thing to say, but I would propose that we have often looked in the wrong places for the main line of English poetry. I do not mean that we have looked to the wrong poets, though there have been serious omissions; but in looking for poetry that resembles Donne-via-Eliot, we lose sight of some of the greatest English poems, as we lose sight of their Englishness. We have looked out for the dramatic suddenness and vibrancy of *The Good-Morrow*, and we have missed what Sir Henry Wootton described (in 1600) as the poetry of 'passionate plainness'. It is a fine phrase. It suggests the dense, sturdy forcefulness and deliberate clarity of poets we think of as characteristically English: Ralegh, Ben Jonson, Charles Churchill, Dr. Johnson, Crabbe, Wordsworth, Keats, Thomas Hardy. I am aware that it is a slippery business talking about one's national identity, and that it may give grounds for all kinds of undesirable flag-wagging. But when all the qualifications are made, there is an unmistakable anatomy to our national literature, and it is worth sorting and judging if we are to understand our place in history, and the nature of our values now. For the Elizabethan poets forged the central style of English poetry. The work cost a good deal in human and literary effort; it took about fifty years to complete, to hand on the techniques, the modes of thought, feeling and expression which would provide a sufficient frame of reference for the poets of the next three centuries. In sum, the Elizabethans perfected the short poem, and they made a great many strong and beautiful poems in doing so. It is the purpose of this book to find those poems. By and large, we don't find them. We think of Elizabethan poets as, at best, like Sir Philip Sidney in his most charming and iridescent effects, and otherwise (which is to say most of the time) as stale, banal, overdecorated and flimsy. We

10

learn to spot the tricks of Sidneyishness in order to say of a poem, not that it is good or bad, but that it is Sidneyish, and as such inferior to Donne, whose Donneishness we may think of as made up of pyrotechnics and insolence. But suppose our first encounter with the poetry of Donne's time were not with *The Good-Morrow* or *The Sun Rising*, but with this:

Those pretty wrongs that liberty commits,
When I am sometime absent from my heart,
Thy beauty and thy years full well befits,
For still temptation follows where thou art.
Gentle thou art, and therefore to be won,
Beauteous thou art, therefore to be assailed;
And when a woman woos, what woman's son
Will sourly leave her till she hath prevailed?
Ay me! but yet thou mightst my seat forbear,
And chide thy beauty and thy straying youth,
Who lead thee in their riot even there
Where thou art forced to break a twofold truth,
    Hers, by thy beauty tempting her to thee,
    Thine, by thy beauty being false to me.

We might, unwarily, find the lines predictably regular, the form over-rigorous, the metaphors conventional and so on. If so, we would have missed the lovely level movement of the pentameter, the tiny changes which register shifts of intense feeling, the strength and elegance of this clear language, the subtle, accurate syntax. This is Shakespeare's 41st sonnet, and it demonstrates the power and command of Elizabethan poetry, of a style near perfection. Such a mixture of calm and terror, such firmness and precision of movement demand a lengthy and arduous training; the roughness and irregularity of one portion of Donne's poetry is not 'harder' or more 'real' than Shakespeare's sonnets or Jonson's Elegies. It is always hard to write like a Jonson. As a start to understanding this, it will be as well to consider the historical situation, the culture and ideologies, the training and education which led to the flowering of Elizabethan poetry, and the definition of that sturdiest literary form, the short poem.

THE HISTORY

It is never easy to suggest in a few paragraphs some of the essential pressures which compose an historical climate. Probably one should concentrate on the economics of a time, and on its political ideologies. Certainly we have left behind the recitation of kings and battles—'drum and sceptre history', once staple school fare. The economics and ideologies of 16th-century England polarise overwhelmingly about a single point: the Court; and historical summary is bound to discuss the Court and its influence almost exclusively.

England settled into its exuberant nationalism with the establishment of Tudor stability. Henry VII set out the great commonplaces of Tudor politics to the satisfaction of the feudal dynasties in York and Lancaster, torn open by a century of sporadic, aimless combat and discontent. Henry VIII brought a different kind of satisfaction and restlessness; to a real extent he animated and extended the intellectual life of the country. He provided, late and slowly, for the opening of England to the force of the Renaissance. The change is visible in the houses. English domestic architecture begins to flower in the 16th century. The fortifications disappear; new wings cross the ancient moats; the deer parks become gardens; a colonising horticulture takes possession of still virgin heath. Nor was it only the great houses that grew fat. The yeoman farmers rebuilt and extended *their* houses; the Elizabethan farmhouse became a striking addition to the English landscape; the rise of the gentry had begun. This growth, swelling on a great wave of economic prosperity, surged most strongly forward upon the consumption of the monastic lands. Where a locality had revolved upon its monastery for its vital centre, it now revolved upon its great house, and that house revolved upon the Court. The social structure of the countryside was redistributed, and the Court became for the first time in England fully the intellectual, moral, and fashionable metropolis of the land. Now this must mean a great deal to a poet. The Court provides him with an audience, intelligent, cultivated, leisurely; it provides a set of shared assumptions and moral standards, implicit but known to be there; most importantly, it provides a language and a code of behaviour. Literally, it teaches 'courtesy'. The significance of this will, I hope, come out in the discussion of particular poets later on, but the point needs emphasis today, when we are apt to feel that the Elizabethan Court was only a more dressy version of our own irrelevant royalty. One could suggest that the nearest a poet might find to a Court today is the University, and in so far as the University patronises, commissions, and encourages artistic dialogue and creation, then maybe it isn't a bad patron. A poet—or any creative artist—needs a centre of collaboration as much as he needs a sense of his own lonely uniqueness. Since the Romantics, we have underemphasised the collaboration, the urgent need for a Court.

But to talk in this way quickly tends to idealisation. The Court of Henry VIII gave its dynamic impulse to society, but it was not only dangerous, authoritarian and unpredictable (slight and frivolous misdemeanours could lead to banishment, or even execution); it was at points boorish, philistine, or merely vulgar. The consolidation and refining of English poetry through the century is exactly recorded in the increasing sophistication and sanity of the Court under Elizabeth—and hers was by no means free from brutality and squalor. None the less, the Court was there, at its best a fertile and civilising force. Further, it provided a model also for the great houses which sprang up so profusely in the Home Counties and the West Country; the best of the Court throve most vigorously at Wilton House and Penshurst. Jonson's great poem (see p. 153) makes the matter clear.

There is, therefore, no doubt that economic prosperity, the Court, and literature are intimately linked together. The great Renaissance courts sucked enormous profits from Africa, Asia, and the Americas. England was late on the scene, and a fairly minor contributor until well into the 17th century, but her extremely efficient commercial navy, buccaneering, and a less repressive social structure than in Spain or France, made for high economic success. Lavish and flagrant buildings began to abound, founded on ruthless exploitations of slave-labour and raw materials or on piracy; Burghley's swaggering showpiece, Wootton Lodge, Wollaton, Longleat, Compton Wynyates, Audley End, Hatfield, Hardwick, Hampton Court itself, all these were manured by American bullion and Asian trade. The booming economy was sustained at home: rising prices, new enterprises, both agrarian and industrial, rising population and production, held a balance and provided for the birth of the handsome, spacious market towns of Wiltshire or East Anglia, plump on their own good mutton and grain. The boom blew open a few bankrupts; there were casualties. But largely the prosperity offered every chance for showiness, for grand households, for cultivation and civilised argument, for educational change and inventiveness, for study. And given the greater mobility of English society, more wealth became diffused through society: instead of 5 per cent, it was available to 10 per cent; instead of power concentrated in the hands of the landed class, it shifted to include the new and prestigious professionals—lawyers, teachers, poets, merchants. It is worth adding that out of a population of about three and a half million towards the end of the 16th century, a thousand families had incomes of £1,000 per annum or more—perhaps the equivalent today of £15,000. Both figures are astonishingly high.

The foregoing remarks on economic conditions do something to suggest their importance to any literary study. But of course it was not only money which created the sumptuousness of the Renaissance Court. The multiplying bureaucracy, the wastefulness, the extravagance, the diligent and serious-minded writing, the schools and universities, were all prompted by new, fierce visions of society. These visions consumed the money.

THE INTELLECTUAL CONTEXT

The most spectacular intellectual movement was Protestantism. Henry VIII shrewdly rode its crest in order to effect his divorce, but the ground-surge would have swept through without him, and Mary only occupied an irrelevant, blood-stained parenthesis.

The two ideological forces which crossed and swirled through the century, the Reformation and the Catholic Counter-Reformation, may be seen as issuing in a single intellectual tradition—that of Renaissance Humanism. To say this is to blot out huge complexities and savage heroisms: for example, the poet Robert Southwell who sought out martyrdom in order to insist on the contrary energy of the Counter-Reformation. The variety and tempests should transpire in the poetry to come. Yet in spite of the variety, the vision of Humanism seems to shake itself clear of contention, and to burn steadily above the quarrels. We are still pupils to that light, and it informs the best minds of its age, as well as—however altered and obscured—of our own. It needs a closer scrutiny.

The most powerful intellectual impetus to the Renaissance in England thrust from the classics. A simple count of the translations which became available between 1500 and 1550 confirms this. And there are two men whose stature and influence are incontestable, and who may be taken to represent in its early English days the finest part of the Humanist tradition: Erasmus and Sir Thomas More. These two men, Erasmus a Dutchman and More, to become a martyr to his own sense of moral alienation, are different in much, but they cleared away a great deal of rubbish for the benefit of later writers, and they defined a tradition for men to work from.

It is the latter point we should understand. Every writer needs a sense of the past, of the way in which past standards, rhythms, voices, work in him and send him to find his own voice. It is a matter of continuity. A man without continuity is without memory, and so, he is crazy. One's memory of people and experiences known, and hence of books known, shapes one's life moment by moment, and until these relations are faced and sorted, it is hard to make sense of that life. Now Erasmus and More found an English language more or less without shape or lineage, and they also found that ancient literature spoke to their profoundest sense of their own life and times. Their problem was to bring together the times and the ancient literature in such a way as to provide for the growth, rooted and secure, of a new literature and way of feeling. It is the work of us all and of a lifetime. We take, for example, an institution—grammar schools, say, or trade unions—and, feeling that there is something wrong, try to reform it so as to discard the dead or obnoxious, and retain the vital continuity, the living tradition. It is all exceedingly difficult and delicate. I am an incompetent Latinist, and cannot therefore trace the interaction between these two men and classical literature, but our own experiences may provide a usable analogy when we have ourselves encountered a writer from the past whose work, though set fast in a different age, has so entered and possessed our minds and spirits that he compels us to revise our values on his terms. Thus continuity holds on, and the past moves in the present. This is what happened to More and Erasmus, but the event was the more momentous in that they became the spokesmen of the English Renaissance. More's *Utopia* (1516) is a noble casebook of Renaissance Humanist attitudes, and Erasmus's *Praise of Folly* (1506) is a robust, boisterous sample of its best (and serious) humour. Together, the two books set a touchstone for the civilised minds of the time, and around the two books they group their textbooks, commentaries, translations, and More, his poetry. In an age which abounded in books of behaviour and moral guides, *Utopia* is probably the finest. In it, More deplores the excess and luxury of Renaissance extravagance; he commends instead the gravity, the serene, sweet order of domestic virtues, plain living and building, a humane democracy and clear, unfettered speech. It is a stirring programme. And at the same time, Erasmus urges unfaltering application to the classics, to listing and learning by heart the great masters, to endless and accurate imitation, and the taking to heart of moral lessons. Both men were perfectly clear that that was what the study of literature was about. Literature was for pleasure and instruction, the two were inseparable and together they made for a truthful morality. The position is made hard and definite by Ben Jonson in his magnificent manual *Timber, or Discoveries* (1616), which stands at the further end of our study and provides, in turn, a memorable bill of its principles:

> There cannot be one colour of the mind, another of the wit. If the mind be staid, grave, and composed, the wit is so; that vitiated, the

other is blown, and deflowered . . . we may conclude: wheresoever manners and fashions are corrupted, language is. It imitates the public riot. The excess of feasts, and apparel, are the notes of a sick State; and the wantonness of language, of a sick mind.

. . . We do not require in [the poet] mere Elocution, or an excellent faculty in verse; but the exact knowledge of all virtues, and their contraries, with ability to render the one loved, the other hated, by his proper embattling them . . .

For a man to write well, there are required three Necessaries. To read the best authors, observe the best speakers, and much exercise of his own style . . . take care in placing, and ranking both matter, and words, that the composition be comely; and to do this with diligence, and often. No matter how slow the style be at first, so it be laboured [at], and accurate: seek the best . . . So did the best Writers in their beginnings; they imposed upon themselves care, and industry. They did nothing rashly. They obtained first to write well, and then custom made it easy, and a habit. By little and little, their matter showed itself to them more plentifully; their words answered, their composition followed; and all, as in a well ordered family, presented itself in the place . . . Besides, as it is fit for grown and able writers to stand of themselves, and work with their own strength, to trust and endeavour by their own faculties: so it is fit for the beginner and learner to study others, and the best. For the mind and memory are more sharply exercised in comprehending another man's things, than our own; and such as accustom themselves and are familiar with the best Authors, shall ever and anon find somewhat of them in themselves, and in the expression of their minds, even when they feel it not, be able to utter something like theirs, which hath an authority above their own. Nay, sometimes it is the reward of a man's study, the praise of quoting another man fitly. And though a man be more prone and able for one kind of writing than another, yet he must exercise all. For as in an instrument, so in style, there must be a harmony, and consent of parts.

pp. 593, 595, 615–17

It is a remarkable and beautiful passage. Probably, outside the Bible, no one of the time wrote finer prose than this. It is calm and graceful, and its powerful feeling is masked by its coolness and deliberation. It is Jonson himself that we know as we read, and implicit within the prose is the peculiar genius of his common sense. The style of writing he defines is a moral style: he asks for 'gravity' and 'composure', for a vigorous moral sense; he reproaches Renaissance 'excess' and 'wantonness'; he insists on steady work, on the imitation of the masters, on ordered serenity in language, on 'a harmony, and consent of parts'. The musical metaphor is no accident, nor was Jonson speaking frivolously when he told Drummond that 'Donne should be hanged for not keeping of the accent'. His statements recall the beautiful lines in *Little Gidding* (1943) where Eliot formulates the poetry *Four Quartets* seeks to shore up against the times:

> where every word is at home,
> Taking its place to support the others,
> The word neither diffident nor ostentatious,
> An easy commerce of the old and the new,
> The common word exact without vulgarity,
> The formal word precise but not pedantic,
> The complete consort dancing together.

V, 217–23

'Easy commerce' 'exact' 'formal' 'consort': the words would have suited Jonson. Jonson draws on that rich, abundant Humanism first and most surely set down by More and Erasmus. If it sounds austere, then we forget all that Humanism meant in terms of a gigantic and rebellious eloquence. Our present-day notions of Puritanism derive from an awful debasement of the Puritan spirit, from Praisegod Barebones and Zeal-of-the-Land Busy. Yet More and Jonson were Puritan; that is, they felt a mighty surge towards immersion in the pleasures of life, and a no less powerful tendency towards asceticism and discipline. From this unneurotic tension they charged their lives. More would have endorsed what is written in *Timber*, and the same argument informs all our study of literature, and hence of morality, today. It is worth seeing how the principles worked in Elizabethan education, what was the training given to the poets.

EDUCATION

The dramatic rise in the establishment of grammar schools and university colleges after Henry VIII dissolved the monasteries is partly the result of a need to fill the educational gap left by superannuated monks, and it is also the result of a new need to provide large numbers of officials for the crowd of bureaucrats spawned by court administration and its spendthrift treasury. But the new schools testify most importantly to the energy of Renaissance Humanism, and the suddenness and delight with which Englishmen received its import. Education for the individual, for the Christian gentleman in society, had arrived; men looked to it to perform scarcely fewer miracles than we look for education to provide today. Because of this faith, we may sometimes make an idealised version of the Elizabethan schoolboys' response to the exhausting treadmill they drove ten hours a day, six days a week. All the same, they went through with it, and if there were many who, as now, played private games in the back row or gazed through the window at the girls, there were enough whose intelligences were toughened and tempered by the work, and whose creative energies learnt discretion, discipline, staying-power and tact. This curriculum set out for the Royal Grammar School, Worcester, 1544, is pretty representative:

In the Fourth Form the boys shall be taught to know the Latin syntax readily, and shall be practised in the stories of poets, and familiar letters of learned men, and the like.

In the Fifth Form they shall commit to memory the figures of Latin oratory and the rules for making verses, and at the same time shall be practised in making verses and polishing themes. Then they shall be versed in translating the chastest poets and the best historians.

Lastly, in the Sixth Form they shall be instructed in the formulas of *The Copiousness of Words and Things* written by Erasmus, and learn to master varyings of speech in every mode so that they may acquire the faculty of speaking Latin, as far as is possible for boys. Meanwhile they shall taste Horace, Cicero, and other authors of that class. Meanwhile, they shall compete with one another in declamations so that they may leave well learned in the school of argument.

These classes principally the Head Master shall try to polish in Latin.

He shall come into school by seven o'clock to perform his duty

> of teaching thoroughly. He shall, too, every other day make some
> English sentences into Latin, and teach the flock committed to him
> to change it into many forms.

The pupil worked doggedly through the Vernacular and Vulgate Bibles, for the training was in *Christian* Humanism; and then through Homer; the Latin masters, Ovid, Virgil, Lucan, Juvenal, eventually at the University the erotic poets, Martial, Catullus. Side by side with the poets lay the preceptors and critics: Cicero, Aristotle, Quintilian, Horace; the historians: Sallust, Tacitus, Livy. Finally, the new men, who incorporated the wisdom of the ancients into their sense of living actuality. These were the teachers who made the ancients pressing and relevant to the young Jonson or Shakespeare: after More, Erasmus and Vivès came a host of theoreticians, marking out the ground and its limits—Ascham in *The Schoolmaster*, Cox in *The Art or Craft of Rhetoric*, Day in *The English Secretary*, Fenner in *The Arts of Logic and Rhetoric, plainly set forth in the English Tongue*, Peacham in *The Garden of Eloquence*, Puttenham in *The Art of English Poesie*, and perhaps the most used, Wilson's *Art of Rhetoric*. The great Headmaster of Westminster, Camden, was an immeasurable influence on the host of scholars and poets he taught as boys and men. There were dozens of textbooks; with these in hand, the able pupil and, later, the able undergraduate, learned the three prongs of the *trivium*: Grammar, Logic, Rhetoric, the curricular model of every school from whose central unit the grammar schools took their name. The pupil learned to describe the syntactical structure of a piece of verse, and to note any blemishes; he would attend to the rhetorical figures of speech, to their propriety or their irrelevance, and he would relate their prominence to the prevailing decorum of the poem; he would detect and analyse the stages of the poem's logic, and isolate its errors. He would classify its style, as the high or lofty style, whose purpose was to move and persuade, the middle or florid style, whose purpose was to delight, and the low and plain style, which was simply to teach and tell the truth. The student who stayed the course learned an exact and sensitive discipline, one which had been shaped for two centuries in the medieval universities and had then been regenerated and transformed to meet the demands of the new age. The procedures and the structure of the *trivium* were of a piece with the political and moral beliefs of the century. They were secure, and definite as stone, and yet they allowed for the free play of the mind. They were founded on moral absolutes and divine reason, but they could contain and vitalise paradoxes and scepticism. They gave a vehicle for eloquence and for plain speech. Society and its language was poised between the dense, closed finalities of the Middle Ages and the great gusts of revolution which were to come after 1600.

LANGUAGE, THE POETIC TRADITION AND THE SHORT POEM

The stress of this argument has fallen so far and perhaps to some tastes too heavily upon control, exclusion, clarity and rigour of writing. Now these are terms which may sound confined to our ears, and in justice it may be said that spoken language today is too pale and flaccid for us to worry much about severity. As Roy Campbell blew up with a modern poet:

You've got the snaffle and the bit all right,
But where's the bloody horse?

Well, I believe language *can* still be used with Jonsonian lucidity and strength, but that is not the point at issue. What matters is that the Elizabethans were preoccupied with having an unbroken, unsaddled, bucking horse to corral and ride. They had to learn a tough discipline, or their language would, as it often did, run away with them or toss them off its back. Tom Nashe and his journalists, Lyly in his famous and verbose *Euphues* (1578–80) plunged into the prose speech of the day and all sense vanished. The first blank verse tragedies of the 1580s, *King Cambyses* or *The Spanish Tragedy*, are linguistic orgies, they fairly seethe with words. *Love's Labour's Lost* (1594) constructs a delighted parody on the excesses of Elizabethan speech. For the 16th century found out English. At the start it was only a spoken tongue; Sir Thomas More wrote mostly in Latin. Then the translations of manuals and classic poems came tumbling into the libraries, men began to write more and more poems in English, Tyndale's translation of the Bible appeared (1547), Tottel's *Miscellany*, an anthology of contemporary English poems, was published (1557), and the new language had arrived. The ancient classics fertilised and chastened this literary English; they gave order to the heap of words and rhythms gathered from Norman-French, Anglo-Saxon, the medieval schoolmen, and released in the new currents of the Renaissance. As always in linguistic and literary change, it is not so much drastic innovation that needs emphasis as the nature of continuity and transmutation, the way in which old ways of thought and feeling are redistributed by the changing needs. There is no doubt that the 16th century did see enormous changes in language and literature, that the changes were real and permanent, and that we are still heirs to those changes. None the less the past was still visible in the present, the Middle Ages were very audible to the Elizabethans. That is one source of their great strength. One could say that our language is often too conceptual and abstract, as well as being overspecialised and inflexible. Medieval English was, no doubt, often too blunt and choppy, and its conversational habits so far from ours that it may look garrulous and casual. I believe this to be true of Chaucer on many occasions. But the Elizabethans stood between the two tendencies. From medieval poets they learned the strong stresses and heavy caesura of the old alliterative line:

> Sithen cherely to the chapel . choses he the waye,
> Prevely aproched to a prest, . and preyed him there
> That he wolde lifte his lif . and lern him better
> How his saule shulde be saved . when he shulde seye hethen.
>
> SIR GAWAYNE AND THE GREEN KNIGHT, 22 1876–79

The same step treads heavily through George Gascoigne:

> Lo, here the cause for why I take this pain;
> Lo, how I love the wight which doth me hate;
> Lo, thus I lie and restless rest in Bath,
> Whereas I bathe not now in bliss, perdie,
> But boil in bale and scamble thus in scath,
> Because I think on thine inconstancy.
>
> DON BARTHOLOMEW'S DOLOROUS DISCOURSES

From the Morality Plays, from medieval illuminations, from the ringing rhetoric of the medieval pulpit, the Elizabethans learned also to use allegory, to personify moral ideas as living forces; given the new and stirring ideas abroad in their time, allegory lent them a peculiar energy so that in the poetry written between about 1550 and 1660 we can see complex and powerful abstractions moving in poetry with a living force. Falstaff is an example of this. He concentrates a number of traditional moral notions about vice and age and so on, and then he lives them out with his immense energy, so that we feel the moral notions (and their contradictions) as living passions. The same thing happens in the poetry of Fulke Greville.

Alliteration, then, and allegory persisted in and quickened Elizabethan poetry. Then the Elizabethans took over and adapted, perhaps from Chaucer, perhaps from somewhere else, the decasyllabic line, the unkillable English pentameter. Prosody can be a dusty subject, but until we can pick out the ten-syllabic iambic line, in verse and in conversation, we shall remain tone-deaf, unmoved by the loveliest effects. It is a matter of ear and of training. We make pentameters unconsciously every day; listen for them:

> I'll make the coffee if you cut the bread.
> We ought to be in London in an hour.
> Now who the hell has pinched my fountain pen?
> I think he's putting on a lot of weight.
> For God's sake will you stop that awful noise?

and so on. The rhythms are still there in our normal speech, and they always have been. Elizabethan poets found, for example, this verse in a Tudor songbook. It is courtly and it is fairly plain. The rhyme scheme and the ten-syllabic line come originally from *Troilus and Criseyde*; the Elizabethans learned the line, modified it in Italy, and made it the instrument of rigour and of suppleness, flexible and strong, capable either of making statements charged with magnificence or easy and unruffled conversation:

> Alas, it is I that wot not what to say,
> For why I stand as he that is abused;

> There as I trusted I was late cast away,
> And no cause given to be so refused;
> But pity is that trust should be misused
> Other by colour or by false semblance;
> Where that is used can be no surance.

BM FAYRFAX MS 14

These were the traditions and techniques which served the Elizabethan poets. Before closing this section, however, I think it is worth summarising in theoretic terms what I take to be the special virtues of the short poem, which the poets described in this book brought to perfection, which engaged the finest minds of the century and which, Shakespeare's drama apart, produced the greatest results. What is more, the same form has held the attention of poets and students for the subsequent four hundred years. One poet of the time speaks for the way in which the short poem should be written, and his remarks might provide a test on which to base a good deal of our subsequent evaluation. George Gascoigne in his *Certain Notes of Instruction* (1575) says:

> Here by the way I think it not amiss to forewarn you that you thrust as few words of many syllables into your verse as may be; and hereunto I might allege many reasons. First, the most ancient English words are of one syllable, so that the more monosyllables that you use the truer Englishman you shall seem, and the less you shall smell of the inkhorn . . . And as much as you may, frame your style to perspicuity and to be sensible, for the haughty obscure verse doth not much delight, and the verse that is too easy is like a tale of a roasted horse; but let your poem be such as may both delight and draw attentive reading, and therewithal may deliver such matter as be worth the marking.

The recommendations could profit a number of modern poets, and while Gascoigne is certainly speaking up for his own kind of poetry, and there was much beautiful poetry written in more decorated styles than he would have approved of, I think he urges his contemporaries towards the kind of poetry in which English is most triumphant, and which is most fully formed beneath the hands of the masters considered in Chapters 6 and 7: Shakespeare, Greville and Ben Jonson.

The short poem is controlled by logic, a known and regular metre, and generally by rhyme as well. A number of Elizabethans turned to epic, as well as drama, to find a poetry of ampler scope than seemed to be available in the short form. But while it is not the business of this book to consider Spenser's longer poetry, it is at least arguable that he wasted great gifts on *The Faerie Queene*. Allegory on that level is in danger of being too primitive for an intelligent reader who has grown out of knights, damsels and dragons. The short poem can satisfy more exact and realistic demands. It is unhampered by preposterous stories, and by the difficulties which neither Spenser nor Milton wholly overcame of sustaining the poetry through pretty flat narrative country. The short poem retains the power of rhythm and concentrated imagery; it is capable of very powerful general statement whose precision and significance can be pointed and controlled by the poet himself, and not by the demands of his story or the accidents of dramatic liturgy. If the subject-matter be merely slight or descriptive, as in a number of lute songs and madrigals, the poem can be correspondingly brief and may be very attractive. But if the subject be important, then the form—its structure, rhythm, images and details—is considerable enough to bear great matters without pompousness or incongruity. When this occurs we find the greatest works in our literature, which because of the stature of the man who writes them take on in unforgettable brevity a universal relevance. The search for some kind of epic form has spent some great talents. Spenser, Milton, Wordsworth, Pound, T. S. Eliot have devoted much energy away from the short poem and the chance of such absolute command as Jonson won in *To Heaven*, as Greville in the later poems of *Caelica*, as Donne in *Hymn to God the Father* or *Valediction, of my Name, in the Window*, as Shakespeare in *Sonnet 73*. And if it is objected that a short poem is too brief to compass a range of experience, that language cannot do so much in a short space, however great the genius, then the poet can use a sequence of short poems, each complete but interwoven, to expound his growth. Shakespeare's *Sonnets* group themselves in a number of sequences, Greville and Sidney similarly write sonnet-sequences, Donne takes *The Litany*,

George Herbert develops his theme around *The Temple*; later, Baudelaire writes *Les Fleurs du Mal* and Tennyson *In Memoriam*. The short poem is entire and sufficiently brief; it is the direct utterance of a single voice, dealing with great or small matters; it can make statements about experience, or it can imply them from description; its great power reposes in its unrivalled combination of passion and understanding, the dense music of thought and feeling realised at once.

MUSIC AND ARCHITECTURE

My earlier mention of the Tudor songbooks needs much fuller development than it can be given here. The song tradition was more fully formed at the start of Henry VIII's reign than the poetic tradition, and it lent a powerful impulse to the energies of Wyatt and a great many writers later in the period. When we feel baffled or amazed by the variety and resourcefulness of verse patterns and rhyme schemes in the Elizabethans, then we should recall the songbooks. The evidence of those books, as the evidence of the plays and the poems, is that speech at the time moved with stronger, more supple and expressive rhythms than ours today. Speech was nearer song, and musical rhythms lay close to the contours of speech. Probably we cannot learn to speak Elizabethan verse until we know the music, and if we cannot speak it, we cannot value it properly. The inflexions and modulations, the shifts from major to minor statements and back, the phrasing, the slight, delicate but vitalising lilts and delays, the bold, urgent declarations, these all were *realised* (i.e. 'made real') and enforced by the poet's musical sense. The same was no doubt as true of the drama and is in some sense true of any poet or reader of poetry. They must have a fine ear. But the Elizabethan poet in particular felt the omnipresence of music, and of dance too. It is worth listening to his music, and it is worth it not only for the sake of the poetry, but also because the music itself is beautiful, and surpasses much of that later music which gets today a fuller hearing. Nor is there any need to be intimidated; Dowland's lute pieces, Byrd's masses, the madrigals, will speak directly to the listener who enjoys (say) *Twelfth Night*, *The Tempest*, or John Donne.

Like various fragments of these writings, and like the architecture also, the music struggles to unify a certain flamboyance and a plain strength. The great religious music of the Middle Ages was largely monodic. That is, a single musical line ordered its progress, and single voices or a single group strove to attain a purity of sound which could identify itself with the purity of God. It is a music of divine aspiration, and the individual soul obliterates the self in impersonal communion. For the medieval mind, music was a part of the Pythagorean science of numbers, and its stages and patterns danced according to their mathematical intervals. The composer calculated the intervals by known and inviolable laws, for music and mathematics were parts of a single vision which saw all creation as beautifully decreed according to a divine, measurable and musical order. Music, therefore, was to the medieval schoolman a means of mystic understanding of divine reason, and the musician's business was so to regulate the patterns of his music that they imitated the measures of the heavens in their inscrutable dance. 16th-century musicians kept up (as who would not?) this belief in the divine power of music, but their music shifted intentions. One of the greatest Elizabethan composers, Orlando Gibbons, wrote, 'It is proportion that beautifies everything, the whole Universe consists of it, and music is measured by it,' and the remark seems to show the persistence of medieval ideas. But Gibbons made an essentially Renaissance kind of music. His music speaks of concord, of groups of voices subtly and sociably entwined, expressing in its rhythms not only a vivid sense of the might of God, but a quick awareness of its human self. In the massive riches of the period, it is hard to know where to turn, what to recommend as illustration. But if the reader will listen to Tallis's mighty 40-part motet *Spem in Alium*, to Byrd's *Five-Part Mass* and his *Great Service*, to the sombre brilliance of Gibbons's anthems and Bull's *In Nomine*, he will have heard a body of music surpassed only by Bach in richness, clarity, and splendour. There is not space here to describe the beauty of the lute and keyboard music of these men and their doughty contemporaries—Tomkins, Weelkes, Farnaby, Dowland, Morley, and a dozen more

—nor to look in any detail at the structure of madrigals, though I include a brief summary in Chapter 5. Here it must be enough to say that this music like any other has its clichés, that according to a composer's temperament the music inclines now to decoration and now to a bony simplicity. But its finest products, and there are a great many, attain a style and a stature whose quality is very like the greatest poetry; it shares that peculiar density of matter, a tough, sinewy style beneath the level, plain tone, a certain deliberation of step, a clarity of statement.

Finally, the qualities of Elizabethan architecture can only be gestured towards. But they are important by way of insisting that one is always audacious and occasionally bigoted in generalising about an age. The Elizabethans were as mixed a bunch as any other, and the best we can do is to appraise the major movements, decide why we admire them, and then take away for our own improvement what it is we need. So the briefest glance at a few of the houses I mentioned earlier: Wollaton, Longleat, Burghley, Wootton Lodge, Hardwick, Audley End, will remind us of the braggartry and ostentation which this account of the Elizabethans has omitted. Yet, again, I would propose that the qualities of the best of them—say, Hardwick and Wootton Lodge—define the same style which two generations worked to make, and which Byrd and Jonson triumphantly mastered. These houses speak of high creative intensity, a vivid sense of drama and daring, of amazing grace and delicacy, and most moving of all, the same upright regularity, the bold, decisive march of a clear, proud spirit which marks the great music and the poetry.

2

The Native Tradition, Italy, and Sir Thomas Wyatt

I have briefly considered some parts of the native tradition in poetry up to the publication by an unknown editor of the anthology known as *Tottel's Miscellany* (1557). There was a strong song-writing tradition, stronger perhaps than the normally poetic one, and there was the attention given to writing, imitating and translating Latin. There were the first attempts to shape the English ten-syllable line with its regular stresses and close links with everyday speech, and there were the surviving but definite links with the medieval tradition. There was also a powerful and secure set of occasions, styles, kinds of vocabulary and form, and of moral attitudes which dictated the nature and manner of any poem, and since these in a loosened but recognisable version survive at least beyond the Romantic poets and may be noticed in action today, it is worth saying something about them. What we are discussing are the tactics available to a poet at a certain time, and at any time these are limited. We congratulate ourselves sometimes at having thrown off the encumbrance of literary conventions, but of course we are deeply conventional in our behaviour. It is a conventional tactic to violate other conventions. In any case, we are usually and rightly happy to work within certain of the conventional limits: we adopt a certain tone and way of arguing when we write a set essay; we write a free verse poem about our own feelings in a townscape, say, but even in so 'personal' a situation, we unconsciously observe conventions in the way we decide on the length of the lines, or obtain images by setting words together in startling combinations. Indeed, the attention we pay to vivid images is itself a convention, and one only in force for the past 150 years or so. And in everyday lives the conventions of common courtesy provide all kinds of ways to express our feelings—when we shake hands, when we kiss, when we pour out a glass of beer or a cup of tea, we sustain in our gestures the movements of past generations, we charge the moment with a certain ceremony, and we affront or delight the other person by the assurance and (maybe) the poise with which we do these things. The most elaborate ceremony of our lives probably surrounds the mingled relationships of love and sexuality—the now dated verb 'courting' has pleasant connotations. Flirtation is and was pretty elaborate in its manœuvres and concealments; the gap between the discotheque and Wimpy bar and the royal court of King Henry VIII isn't as wide as we might suppose. These remarks should indicate how it is that the rituals of Courtly Love, and the poems arising from them hit nearer our own feelings than we allow. Courtly Love was the intricate and riddling game of flirtation devised for mixed company at the medieval courts. It depended upon teasing allusions to suspected, fictitious or real love-affairs, and the attraction of the game lay partly in agreeable shivers of salaciousness, but more in the opportunities it provided for graceful compliments, witty acrostics and guessing puns, for covert insolence or irony, and for expressions of real passion. And the real passion might centre upon loss or upon frustration or (as very often) the passage of time, and take a flirtatious subject merely as the vehicle for a profounder theme. Courtly Love, therefore, can provide the occasion for dignified writing or for jaunty, flippant verse; it can be serious or it can be slight, and it is wrong to feel that its scope is narrow. The range is as wide as that of one human being's passion for another and sometimes, when human passion is used as a metaphor for divine or metaphysical passion, a good deal wider.

In spite of this, it may be conceded that Elizabethan love poetry has had more than its fair share of attention, and I shall propose that a different set of procedures and attitudes, which are found in the most finished versions of the plain style, deserve

30

quite as much attention and give rise to a tradition of poetry which I clumsily name the poetry of moral reflection. Before coming to this, however, we should briefly explore what was the contribution of Italian literature to the poetry of Courtly Love and, disseminated via the love poetry, to the poetry of the great Elizabethans. This appraisal must involve a summary of the achievement of Francesco Petrarch (1304–74).

Petrarch won the acclaim of a very large public in 14th-century Italy by bringing to bear on the neutral blandness of contemporary Courtly Love his powerful individualism, his stirring sense of his own fiery identity. He took the stylised graces of chivalric emblems and vivified them with his Renaissance energy, and he represents not only the vitalising of love poetry but also, for Englishmen, the most dramatic and available unification of Christianity and the classics; he was, in other words, a great Renaissance Humanist. He therefore won fame not only for his poetry, but also for his literary and critical theories, and these called vigorously for the restoration of Ciceronian and Virgilian virtues, for elegance, chastity of form, for musicality of language, stylishness, above all, for decorative eloquence. For him, Rhetoric was the pillar of art, and from his profuse and vociferous pen we hear again the demands for imitation and learning by heart of the classics. Petrarch antedated More and Erasmus, the great pioneers of the Renaissance in England, by well over a century, but he perfected the sonnet in Italian, and in the opulence and copiousness of later Italian literature his was the honoured name, mentor to Boccaccio, Michelangelo and still, when Sir Philip Sidney was a tourist and student in Venice and Padua, hero to Torquato Tasso. Consequently, we speak of the Petrarchan influence in English poetry, which Sir Thomas Wyatt first brought back, in order to describe the novel ease, grace, finish, and suppleness of line which Wyatt and half a dozen writers after him saw as so lacking in much of the native tradition, and sought to acquire from Italy. It is invidious to speak of the Petrarchan and the native poets as though they were neatly discernible. Like any other innovations in language, the Italian methods and influences appear according to the temperament of the poet, and once they were known in England, then they were ineradicable. They were a part of the civilising of the language. On occasion, Italian poems taught the Englishmen to over-decorate and to indulge in elaborate rhetorical devices which strike us as grotesque or merely tedious, though it is worth recalling that the intention in such moments was to be as richly ornate as possible, to command intellectual admiration and wonder.

> Her cheeks are like the blushing cloud,
>   That beautifies Aurora's face,
> Or like the silver crimson shroud,
>   That Phoebus' smiling looks doth grace:
>   Heigh ho, fair Rosalind!
> Her lips are like two budded roses
>   Whom ranks of lilies neighbour nigh,
> Within which bounds she balm encloses,
>   Apt to entice a deity:
>   Heigh ho, would she were mine!
>
>   Thomas Lodge: ROSALIND'S DESCRIPTION

But the lapses and the clichés are only evidence that the poet lacked a critical sense, and not that he should never have read the Italians. Italian helped English to know itself. The later achievement would have been impossible without its help.

Having said this, it remains to describe the principles and occasions of the native poetry and its more characteristic manner, the moral-reflective, and to add that this more rooted tradition (as one would expect) continues to provide the predominant language and rhythms and is, in my view, the first-spring of the greatest successes. The characteristic manner speaks out in a fine poem of William Dunbar's, written in Scotland about the beginning of the 15th century. It does not matter whether later Englishmen knew it, though they knew Dunbar's contemporary Gavin Douglas, so they probably knew this poem. In any case, it embodies the manner and some of the most familiar matter of the native tradition. The poem is called *Lament for the Makaris* (i.e. makers, or poets), takes for structure and theme a logical unit and a moral commonplace, and by the logical stages of illustration and exposition, states an attitude and the poet's feelings towards the attitude. The liturgical response gives each verse the proper resonance and solemnity.

> Our plesaunce heir is all vane glory,
> This fals world is bot transitory,
> The flesche is brukle, the Fend is sle:
> > *Timor mortis conturbat me.*

The statement is baldly familiar. He extends the statement:

> The stait of man dois change, and vary,
> Now sound, now seik, now blith, now sary,
> Now dansand mery, now like to dee:
> > *Timor mortis conturbat me.*

He enumerates the victims of death:

> On to the ded gois all Estatis,
> Princis, Prelotis, and Potestatis,
> Baithe riche and pur of al degre:
> > *Timor mortis conturbat me ...*

> He sparis no lord for his piscence,
> Na clerk for his intelligence;
> His awful strak may no man fle:
> > *Timor mortis conturbat me.*

The terrible weight of the evidence leads 'of forse' to the conclusion of the syllogism:

> Sen he has all my brether tane,
> He will nocht lat me lif alane,
> Of forse I man his nyxt pray be:
> > *Timor mortis conturbat me.*

> Sen for the deid remeid is none,
> Best is that we for ded dispone,
> Eftir our deid that lif may we.
> > *Timor mortis conturbat me.*

[brukle: broken; the Fend: the Devil; Sle: slain; *Timor mortis conturbat me*: terror of death shakes me; piscence: wealth; I man: I must; remeid: rescue; dispone: prepare; eftir: after; lif: live (verb)]

Every proposition is controlled by the logical structure. The exceptions are the refrain, and a few bare phrases like 'awful strak'. Almost every line is impelled by the remembered force of a biblical text, so the propositions became moral common-places. Yet the poem is powerful and moving; its bareness intensifies the power which accumulates in the impassive, relent-less movement, the grave unselfpitying tone, the rigour and severity of the whole. The attitude is dignified and sane, and it typifies the native tradition. The same virtues may be discovered resting on like principles, both of poetry and life, in these poems we shall later consider: Ralegh's *Even Such is Time* (p. 63), Nashe's *In Time of Plague* (p. 56), Jonson's *Farewell to the World* (p. 145). The charge that these virtues and attitudes, however im-pressive, are too narrow and grim to make for great poetry, will be met all in good time. For now, it must do to rejoin that it is always hard to form an attitude to death which is sufficient and dignified, that such an attitude entails a correspondingly sure view of life, and any poetry which arrives at these values with intelligence, and credibly, deserves all the attention we can give.

The native tradition may be found disguised in love songs, and the later poems adapted the Italian sonnet to include its special properties. But it has its proper 'occasions', i.e. times (as for flirtatious love poetry) when certain kinds of poetry, certain forms and styles are the proper ones to use. There are the epitaph, the epigram, the verse-letter, the versified psalm, the hymn, the satire, and so on. Most of these forms will appear as we look at various poems, but we should understand that each one was con-trolled by its own regulations, and that when a poet neglected or transgressed the rules he did so for good reasons, and in the confidence that his audience would take the point. Thus when Wyatt uses the 'occasion' of the seven penitential psalms to offer some theological propositions of his own, he is making an audacious move. Largely, the forms of moral-reflective verse follow the manners we would expect which were set out in the school textbooks. Thus, a satire is a moral and critical com-mentary on the age, modelled on the classic authors, especially Juvenal. A verse-letter is what it appears to be, and its style, correspondingly casual and conversational, fits its occasion. An epitaph is more serious and tightly constructed, but it is brief enough for a headstone. The epigram (undervalued these days) records in neat, concentrated form a moral generalisation, the generality being carried off by its succinctness and edge. It is one of the most frequent forms in Elizabethan poetry, especially in translations, and though now neglected, it is one of the toughest.

I have reviewed the properties of the Elizabethan poet, described his nearest and most influential tradition, the native one, and indicated some of the effects introduced by a study of Italian. Let us proceed to look at the poetry of Sir Thomas Wyatt, and consider with what success he brought the two kinds of writing together, and made out of a profuse but incoherent heap of materials a poetic voice which calls for attention. It is interesting that, while I am sure he rewards that attention, his work does not seem to lead very directly on to the greatness of later men. Wyatt wrote some fine poems and he achieved, in comparative isolation, a remarkable maturity of style and statement, yet few of his immediate successors profited from his efforts, and the exploits of the great Petrarchan sonneteers, men like Sidney, Spenser and the early Greville, though often charming are also flimsy, and give no signs of their authors' having learned what Wyatt had to teach.

SIR THOMAS WYATT

Wyatt was born at Allington Castle in 1503, and proceeded to Court as a junior in 1516. He was an undergraduate at Cambridge, and married young a peer's daughter who was mother to his two children and thereafter consistently unfaithful until Wyatt refused to live with her. We may fairly speculate whether the game of Courtly Love rationalised the gossip of a promiscuous society, or whether it encouraged promiscuity; probably a little of both. What does seem to me true is that Wyatt's poetry speaks out with unmistakable reality against the Court's viciousness and triviality and on behalf of tenderness and decency. His diplomatic reports from his missions to France testify to his uprightness, and so does this letter to his son, dated 1537.

I have nothing to cry and call upon you for but honesty, honesty.

It may be diversely named, but alway it tendeth to one end. And as I wrote to you last, I mean not that honesty that the common sort calleth an honest man: trust me that honest man is as common a name as the name of a good fellow, that is to say, a drunkard, a tavern-haunter, a rioter, a gamer, a waster: so are among the common sort all men honest men that are not known for manifest naughty knaves. Seek not, I pray thee my son, that honesty which appeareth and is not in deed. Be well assured it is no common thing nor no common man's judgment to judge well of honesty, nor is it no common thing to come by; but so much it is the more goodly for that it is so rare and strong. Follow not therefore the common reputation of honesty; if you will seem honest, be honest, or else seem as you are.

Such writing is worlds away from Sunday-school piety. It is plain and direct, full of dignity and hits off perfectly the affectionate, paternal note the letter requires. It is the easy, unselfconscious utterance of a strong, honourable man, and it will serve as a touchstone to the poems.

After his separation from his wife, Wyatt held various posts at Court, was noted for his sprightly participation in light social intercourse, and soon became an active royal agent on secret continental missions; he was once a political prisoner on the King's behalf in Italy, several times a diplomatic envoy, and twice a political prisoner under the King himself. Gossip has it that before she became queen, Anne Boleyn was Wyatt's mistress, and certainly he lived for several years with one of Queen Catherine's ladies. Wyatt, therefore, like every considerable poet after him, worked at the centre of the country's life. He was a courtier, diplomat, poet, Member of Parliament, and at the time of his death was superintending the building of a new fleet of which he was to be Vice-Admiral. The effect of this central participation in the great affairs of the day is immeasurable, but it was potent, and it is notable that Marvell was probably the last great English poet who was also a leading politician. The results of this separation of politics and literature since the Restoration upon the language of political argument (to look no further) have been very depressing.

Wyatt is probably best known for his love lyrics, but there are fine things in his *Satires* and in the *Penitential Psalms*, and in the love poems it seems to me that we get his best and most characteristic effects when he can shift from the usual postures of love poetry into an attitude and a tone of voice which belong to a fuller, more disenchanted matter-of-fact humanity than a playful situation can express. Such a lyric as this:

> Is it possible
> That so high debate,
> So sharp, so sore, and of such rate,
> Should end so soon and was begun so late?
> Is it possible?
>
> Is it possible
> So cruel intent,
> So hasty heat and so soon spent,
> From love to hate and thence for to relent?
> Is it possible?
>
> Is it possible
> To spy it in an eye
> That turns as oft as chance on die?
> The truth whereof can any try?
> Is it possible?
>
> Is it possible
> For to turn so oft
> To bring that lowest that was most aloft,
> And to fall highest, yet to light soft?
> It is possible!
>
> All is possible,
> Who so list believe;
> Trust therefore first, and after prove,
> As men wed ladies by licence and leave:
> All is possible.

The Petrarchan properties feature in this poem: religion, quarrels, fickle natures, a wanton glance, but these are more than stage properties; they are the actualities and accusations of every love affair. Moreover, the bare language, the absence of imagery, indeed of any developed figure, the fragile delicate stanza-forms remove the poem from the passion of a particular experience, and give it a more generalised position. The style lifts the poem to a place from which it commands a part of all experience; it comments on the bitterness and the loss attendant on any disrupted relationship. It may put us in mind of Hardy. The repetition of the question at every stanza-end not only returns each stanza to a closed shape, it also sustains a rising note of incredulity through the poem until, to our shock, we encounter the grim transposition, 'It is possible'. Wyatt clinches the uncompromising grimness with the grander, sardonic statement of the last stanza, 'All is possible', and edges the generalisation with the bitter two lines, 'Trust therefore first, and after prove,/As men wed ladies by licence and leave' (pronounce *licènce*, as in French). The poem displays, at this remarkably early stage, a technical adroitness and a tactful ear, and it indicates many of Wyatt's gifts: his spare tone and diction, his matter-of-factness, his humanity and the calm, rather set quality of his disenchantment. The poem plays in a minor key, but it has no flaws; it rings true.

There are two other love poems which show off some of Wyatt's range, and suggest also a comparison which illuminates them both: the love poetry of John Donne. For while Wyatt does not possess so mobile, excited and brilliant a mind as Donne, neither is he liable to the master's very peculiar brand of bad taste. The Petrarchan vocabulary gave Donne ample chance to unleash his extravagant imagination. When he denies himself that dazzling excess then he writes in a style which is like the best of Wyatt. But this is only to say what will be said several times more in this book, that the best poems of the period have more in common with each other and less in common with 'Elizabethanness' or 'Petrarchanism'. You cannot value poetry in terms of historical typicality, of schools and revolutions; you can only find the best poems. What Wyatt shows in this next poem may be compared to Donne, and if we rebuke the poem for a deficiency in bright images, and a monotony of metre, then we are missing the rightness of its length, its small, ironic shifts of tone, its compelling truculence. Once more, the poem begins with a conventional situation, but it comments pungently on all broken love affairs, whether Courtly Love games or not, and it attains a just and comical end. It is slighter than *Is it possible?* but only a skilled poet could have written it.

Hate whom ye list, for I care not.
Love whom ye list and spare not.
Do what ye list and dread not.
Think what ye list, I fear not.
For as for me I am not,
But even as one that recks not
Whether ye hate or hate not,
For in your love I dote not:
Wherefore I pray you forget not,
But love whom ye list; for I care not.

The repetition of the grammatical unit in each line is a conscious and jocular device, and the whole thing is held together by its logical structure ('Hate . . . Love . . . Do . . . Think . . . As for me . . . Wherefore . . .', and the clinching last line). Once more, there is no distraction (or ambiguity) lent by imagery, and the changes in metre, though essential, are almost inaudible. And the statements are too forceful to be monotonous; regularity is not at all the same thing as monotony, as Shakespeare's sonnets triumphantly prove.

Wyatt wrote many lovely poems about love, and we cannot take them all. I would urge the reader to turn up *I Have Sought Long; My Pen, Take Pain; Madame, Withouten Many Words*; the candid and beautiful *Perdie, I Said It Not*; *My Lute, Awake*; *Your Looks So Often Cast* and the fine *Blame Not My Lute*. One poem, notable for its rare recollection of a tender and successful relationship, is *They Flee From Me*. I quote the second stanza; the first stanza regrets that his past mistresses now turn from him.

Thankéd be fortune, it hath been otherwise
Twenty times better; but once in special,
In thin array, after a pleasant guise,
When her loose gown from her shoulders did fall,
And she me caught in her arms long and small,

39

> Therewith all sweetly did me kiss,
> And softly said, 'Dear heart, how like you this?'

There is a glad affection here which resists any idea that Wyatt was a wencher. Also, since the evidence abounds of his skill in controlling rhythm, the abrupt, impatient movement must have been what he wanted. That too looks forward to Donne, notably in the soft phrase 'arms long and small', and the gentle, liquid movement of the last two lines. It is an accident, I would guess, of misfortune and not of temperament that Wyatt wrote no poems which celebrate the solidity of a long and stable relationship.

Consequently, although they too are largely poems about harshness, loss, self-reproach, sharp admonitions to the world, his poems of moral reflection about state affairs and religion seem to show where his concerns and his intelligence are most fully engaged. His best love lyrics are about something more than love affairs, and although love poems treat (goodness knows) sufficiently serious subjects, it is this something more which when we find it is the real reward Wyatt yields.

The following poem on the unpredictability of political life is a fiercer business than we have yet encountered.

> Stand who so list upon the slipper top
> Of court's estates, and let me hear rejoice;
> And use me quiet without let or stop,
> Unknown in court, that hath such brackish joys:
> In hidden place, so let my days forth pass,
> That when my years be done, withouten noise,
> I may die aged after the common trace.
> For him death grippeth right hard by the crop
> That is much known of other; and of himself, alas,
> Doth die unknown, dazéd with dreadful face.

The poem is a translation from a passage in one of Seneca's plays, the Latin playwright whose thunderous gloom about political machinations so much caught the Elizabethan imagination. But the poem is more than 'just translation'. It is more what a modern poet, Robert Lowell, has called 'imitation'; that is to say, the recreation within the terms of the first text of an original experience. It is the fertilising of new life by the old, the contiguity of tradition and the present. For there is no doubt that Wyatt feels the original situation as vividly present, and one may guess that the occasion for the poem was some horrifying moment in his political life, maybe a public execution. The poem begins abruptly and dramatically, as many of Wyatt's do, though this is commonly overlooked when the Elizabethan poets are criticised for staleness. There is strong contempt in the compressed, throw-away opening, and in the vivid 'brackish joys'; there is fierce terror in that bold line, 'For him death grippeth right hard by the crop', and this tightness Wyatt momentarily releases as he contemplates the death of the celebrated personage, known to everyone, unknown by himself. The pressure rises again in the last grim phrase, hammered out by the 'd's. It is a poem of individual urgency vitalising a universal theme, no less true now than then. The desperate instability of political life at any time is the theme of his best sonnet, 'The pillar perished is whereto I lent', which it is pretty certain was written after the execution of his close friend and patron, Chancellor Thomas Cromwell, an execution Wyatt had to attend and at which, an eyewitness reports, Cromwell appealed to Wyatt for his prayers, and Wyatt broke down. Once more, the starting point for Wyatt is a translation, this time one of Petrarch's sonnets, but the result, though it has its clichés in the second quatrain, is stamped with Wyatt's qualities of mind and technique. He uses some of the Petrarchan vocabulary, but the native tradition—the alliteration, the bold, phrasal movement, the grim acceptance of pain—makes the poem.

> My pen in plaint, my voice in careful cry:
> My mind in woe, my body full of smart,
> And I myself, myself always to hate,
> Till dreadful death do ease my doleful state.

The moral generalisations arise easily from his particular suffering, and it is this generalising that Wyatt does best. It may sound a gloomy gift. Well, so it is, but its power is real, and Wyatt gives to the passages which best show off his gifts, a deliberate weight, a steadiness of movement, and so completely *realises* his own exceptional truthfulness in this verse that he attains a kind of beauty of moral forthrightness. The beauty (if that's the word) comes out in *If Thou Wilt Mighty Be*. The last verse is probably the most finished, though it is the climax of a solid and powerful poem.

> All were it so thou had a flood of gold
> Unto thy thirst, yet should it not suffice;
> And though with Indian stones (a thousandfold
> More precious than can thyself devise)
> Ychargéd were thy back, thy covertise
> And busy biting yet should never let
> Thy wretched life, ne do thy death profet.

Once more, Wyatt sets out a moral statement with dignity and point; 'blunt' isn't quite the word because the tone is right. He does not here have any of the surliness which sometimes mars the poets in the next chapter, and Wyatt himself elsewhere. The rhythm is even, but the voice moves over the line-endings, gives the verse momentum and the quickness of speech, and permits the placing, bleak and uncompromising, of the closing clause 'ne do thy death profet' (i.e. 'nor do it any advantage').

Wyatt's most accomplished poems no doubt lie amongst those I have considered or listed, but it would be unfair to finish with him without further mention of the *Satires* or the *Penitential Psalms*. The Satire was a form used by most of these poets. It was addressed to a friend and took the form of a homily on moral behaviour, generally with asides on contemporary abuses. Donne's *Satire: of Religion* is probably the best known of its kind. The form provides an easy, conversational tone, a portmanteau for anecdotes and commentary of all kinds, and a more careless, discursive manner and metre than usual. Wyatt's *Second Satire* to John Poynz which tells the old folk fable of the town mouse and the country mouse is interesting for the way in which it prompts comparison with Chaucer rather than Donne. Its rapid, racy narration gives off a salty medieval air, in spite of the innovating rhyme scheme (*terza rima*).

> 'My sister' (quoth she) 'hath a living good,

'And hence from me she dwelleth not a mile.
In cold and storm she lieth warm and dry
In bed of down, and dirt doth not defile

'Her tender foot, she laboureth not as I.
Richly she feedeth and at the rich man's cost,
And for her meat she needs not crave nor cry.'

18–24

After the fable, Wyatt closes the poem with firm and admonitory commonplaces.

The *Penitential Psalms*, written late in 1540, are probably Wyatt's most ambitious effort. Once more, the procedure he chose had classical and Italian precedents, and again he started out in various passages with an argument modelled closely on the original. But the result is unquestionably Wyatt's own voice. The sequence develops by taking a particular psalm to mark a stage in a formal exercise in repentance and religious meditation —a discipline more completely reviewed in the discussion of Robert Southwell (p. 80). Each paraphrase and commentary on the psalm is linked by a brief narrative describing the psalmist's situation. The psalms themselves are not even performances, though there are fine passages in the third (*Psalm* 38) and sixth (130, *De Profundis Clamavi*), but in my judgment the fourth (51, *Miserere Mei*) is the most sustained and finished. Though the appropriate style for these poems would be lofty, partly the quiet and humility necessary to the *Miserere*, partly Wyatt's cast of mind assimilate the poem to his familiar manner—the bony diction, the level movement, the absence of imagery, that steady contemplation of the object of the poem without distraction or frivolity. In its best lines, the poem comes near to Donne's *Hymn to God the Father*.

Rue on me, lord, for thy goodness and grace,
That of thy nature art so bountiful,
For that goodness that in the world doth brace
Repugnant natures in quiet wonderful;
And for thy mercies' number without end
In heaven and earth perceived so plentiful
That over all they do themselves extend:

For these mercies much more than man can sin
Do way my sins that so thy grace offend.
Again wash me, but wash me well within,
And from my sin that thus makes me afraid
Make thou me clean, as ay thy wont hath been.
For unto thee no number can be laid
For to prescribe remissions of offence
In hearts returned, as thou thyself has said.
And I beknow my fault, my negligence,
And in my sight my sin is fixéd fast,
Thereof to have more perfect penitence.

1–18

The movement is grave, the rhythm perfectly adjusted to what is being said. The language is close to liturgy, but it keeps the reader aware of a living voice speaking it (like the best religious music), and the power of the whole poem depends more on the poet's ungrovelling sense of shortcoming and negligence, and the relation of his faults to the best possibilities of life and death, than it depends on an accepted body of theological doctrine. The problem arises in many more poems discussed in these pages: what does the non-believer do with Christian poetry? I have proposed an answer. A sound literature depends for its health on an attitude to life which celebrates the possibilities of life, which can move beyond merely individual responses to some larger impersonality, and which provides in its equivalent attitude to death justification for continuing to live intelligently and well. Such an attitude is religious in a wholly non-sectarian way and without it, one would guess, the creative impulse in men must be stilled, and only destructive forces remain. Wyatt's poem, like the greater religious verse of Donne or Jonson, speaks of this essential experience, and speaks of it to any moral man, Christian or not.

Wyatt's poem is striking and original. If it is not in the first rank, then that is partly because the instruments needed were still in a primitive state, and partly because he lacked a sufficiently mobile mind and the piercing feelings we respond to in Shakespeare's sonnets. And he lacked the grandness of moral vision which we find in a comparable poet, Fulke Greville. In his lyrics, he falls back rather often on lutanists' clichés such as the refrain after every stanza ('Blame not my lute' 'Disdain me not'), and he is sometimes clumsy as medieval poets (including Chaucer) are clumsy, padding lines with 'eke' 'I wis', with archaic inversions ('quiet wonderful'), and rather juvenile phrasing ('thou break/ My strings in spite with great disdain'). A number of rhetorical tricks turn up too often (the 'hap/unhap' antithesis for example). But Wyatt's is a strong voice, direct, real, and fully formed. I take him every bit as seriously as (say) Henry Vaughan, or in this century, Robert Frost.

POSTSCRIPT: SKELTON, MORE, SURREY

I have placed Wyatt as the first poet of the period who deserves study in detail. As a matter of historical justice, I should mention these three poets, though the account will be scanty. Skelton died in 1529, an internationally known scholar, and a Latin poet. He also wrote a native verse, heavily alliterative and largely written in a brief, jerky metre, which has its moments. The influence of More as scholar and prose-writer (and of course as politician) we have seen; he also wrote round about the turn of the century some moral-reflective verse which is unremarkable but decent. Surrey is a harder case to fix in a couple of sentences. Certainly lesser than Wyatt, he none the less took on the work of creating an English style, and wrote a smooth pentameter more to the taste of *Tottel's* readers than much of Wyatt. Apart from Vaux, he is probably the best in the ruck of mediocrities between Wyatt and Gascoigne. Habitually, he is prolix and conventional in the wrong way, but the reader should turn up his biting sonnet on Henry VIII, *Sardanapalus*, and the nostalgic poem *So Cruel Prison* on Windsor Castle, written during one of his imprisonments before his execution for treason.

3

The Plain Blunt Men: Vaux, Gascoigne, Nashe and Ralegh

These poets worked exclusively in the native tradition. Two of them, Gascoigne and Ralegh, bring the potentialities of that tradition to a high pitch of achievement, and the other two, together with Barnabe Googe and George Turberville who are crowded out by lack of space, wrote some pungent poems in the native manner. The work of these men is not really contingent upon Wyatt's, because Wyatt was a pioneer and an experimenter, at points impatient and dissatisfied with the English poetic speech he found, and ambitious of creating something with a more flexible range of perception. And he was working by himself, in an environment often vulgar and brutal, and always lacking the self-confidence and comfortable wealth which made Elizabeth's Court a much easier place to work in, and the similar job Sidney was later to set himself less solitary and immense. Wyatt accomplished remarkable things, as I have argued, and the unevenness of his poetry is partly due to his situation and partly to his ambitions. The writers we consider here are more limited than Wyatt, and more at home with the speech their lives and reading provided. They did not feel as Sidney was to feel that the language was uncivil and primitive, and they were much less interested in the love songs than in homiletics—the persistent medieval tradition of moral reflection and Christian resignation. Thus they found it congenial to remain within the habits of the native manner, to rely upon its tried sequences of moral statement, logical development, the regular insistence of its rhythms and the steady, confident return to the rhyme-ending. And the method lived up to the new demands. Gascoigne and Ralegh in particular raised this kind of writing to a rare intensity and succinctness; they brought about a union of compression and understatement requiring organisation and discipline of a very high order and which provides the unseen but essential basis on which the later poets built. Rhyme, rhythm, syntax and logical structure, tone and manner coalesce and solidify as a style, powerful enough for the great (Jonson, Shakespeare), minute and lissom enough for the slight and stylish (Morley, Herrick).

The significance of Ralegh and Gascoigne is more than historical; they perfected the style and they wrote fine poems. Their range is not wide nor their feeling ample, but they concern themselves with the central issues of experience and they touch familiar and commonplace experience to vivid life by the force and resolution of their writing. Thomas, Lord Vaux, a much lesser writer than these two, is a convenient early example of native writing. We have looked at Dunbar's *Lament for the Makaris*, and it is worth turning up in *The Oxford Book of 15th Century Verse* the beautiful brief poem which begins

A God and yet a man?
A maid and yet a mother?
Wit wonders what wit can
Conceive this or the other.

Vaux's few poems make clear the way in which this kind of writing held through (may still hold now). Their virtues embody in a useful and obvious way the elemental qualities of the native style, mobilised by a limited writer at a primitive stage. Although he is limited in execution and grasp, his themes are large ones, and he can allow customary metres and conventions to reinforce the modesty of his insight. The grave, steady metre, the serious theme, redeem the smaller poetry of the Elizabethans as their verse and subjects do not redeem the smaller Romantic poets (such as Thomas Moore) or those of our own day. Which is not to say that there were no Elizabethan poetasters—*Tottel's Miscellany* has plenty of turgid, monotonous rubbish in it—but that a poet like Vaux, fairly intelligent but cautious and restricted, could rely on the traditions he found in operation, and make an honest job of it. For the Elizabethan, there was no agonising need as for Eliot to say:

> And so each venture
> Is a new beginning, a raid on the inarticulate
> With shabby equipment always deteriorating
> In the general mess of imprecision of feeling,
> Undisciplined squads of emotion.

EAST COKER, 178–82

Perhaps it is worth asking whether the modern movement has not too hastily relinquished the traditional metres and manners. I like this following poem of Vaux's *because* its metre is regular, its rhyme unmistakable, imagery absent, its statements pithy and declarative. The poem is called *The Aged Lover Renounceth Love*; it is a selfconscious 'occasion' (there is an analogous Latin poem by Catullus) for which the plain style is suitable. It is interesting that the poem was set to music, widely known, and sung by Shakespeare's grave-diggers in *Hamlet* V, *i*, half a century later.

> I loathe that I did love,
>   In youth that I thought sweet,
> As time requires for my behove,
>   Methinks they are not meet.

> My lusts they do me leave,
>   My fancies all be fled,
> And tract of time begins to weave
>   Grey hairs upon my head.

What gives the poem its edge and justifies the monotone is the relentless pressure of feeling and idea towards the end, which is death. The poem is not trite because the statements are so unanswerably bare, the tone so wintry, and when we look closer, the subdued alliteration, the tiny releases of line-ending vary and thrust on the exposition.

> The harbinger of death,
>   To me I see him ride;
> The cough, the cold, the gasping breath
>   Doth bid me to provide.

At the end, the poem rounds on its reader, and with unmetaphor-ical bleakness bids him remember his end.

> And ye that bide behind,
>   Have ye none other trust:
> As ye of clay were cast by kind,
>   So shall ye waste to dust.

Vaux exposes in simple, sometimes mechanical operation the elements of the native style. The subject is broad and proverbial, brought to life by the austerity and bluntness of the man.

GASCOIGNE

In Gascoigne, similarly broad themes move into life beneath the roughness of his curious truculence of voice. Bluntness, trucu-lence, rough dignity—these may seem odd things to commend a poet for, but they are unmistakable qualities and we may find them in some withdrawn but valuable men. Remember, and weigh Wordsworth's definition of a poet, and we shall apply it to Gascoigne and Ralegh.

> He is a man speaking to men: a man, it is true, endued with more lively sensibility, more enthusiasm and tenderness, who has a greater knowledge of human nature, and a more comprehensive soul, than are supposed to be common among mankind . . . [his] object is truth, not individual and local, but general, and operative . . . truth which is its own testimony, which gives strength and div-inity to the tribunal to which it appeals, and receives them from the same tribunal.
>
> Preface to LYRICAL BALLADS

This force and penetration can manifest itself in many ways, not necessarily bardic, difficult, and oracular ways. The way may be argumentative and direct. It is no accident that the central methods of the mighty line of English (and Scottish) philosophers have been sceptical, matter-of-fact, ironic, cautious, everyday. Some of the same methods and habits direct one course of English poetry; they compose the native style. It *is* a style, assured, explicit and describable, and Gascoigne is a notable representa-tive. There is no point in inflating his achievement, but his work is scarcely read at all nowadays, though it was admired by his contemporaries, and it may help to suggest that amongst those contemporaries Gascoigne's short poems easily surpass those of, say, Drayton or Daniel, and in a longer perspective, those of serious and capable poets like Goldsmith or Matthew Arnold.

Gascoigne's love poems, though nominally Petrarchan efforts, use very little of the courtly diction and almost always get away from the initiating theme towards moral reflection. Like a composer who takes a melody as the vehicle for his tenor variations and departures, Gascoigne's moves from Courtly Love to moral aphorism. Sometimes Courtly Love provides the metaphors for a moral poem, as in *Lullaby of a Lover*, where Gascoigne bids to sleep all those distractions which keep him from Christian resignation. Here, as often in Gascoigne, the lines mark off the premisses of the argument, while their brevity gives that argument grimness and finality. It is Vaux's procedure advanced with greater dignity and accomplishment. The fourth verse is one of the most memorable in its union of strange, rough courage with discomposing moral truisms.

> And lullaby, my wanton will:
> Let reason's rule now reign thy thought,
> Since all too late I find by skill
> How dear I have thy fancies bought;
> With lullaby now take thine ease,
> With lullaby thy doubts appease.
> For trust to this: if thou be still,
> My body shall obey thy will.

The strength of this is not merely that Christian stoicism is no longer familiar to us; the strength is Gascoigne's—his hardness of statement and sternness of feature. The effect arises partly from the control of slight alliteration won from the medieval poets, partly from the shift in rhyme pattern which enforces the two closing sentences, and partly from the way in which the line lengths denote the stages of the argument and march the poem inevitably to its end. The only rhetorical figure is the repetition

of 'lullaby', a word which is at sardonic odds with its usual associations, though the image of sleep for death is as old as Christen-
dom. The poem ends:

> Thus lullaby, my youth, mine eyes,
> My will, my ware, and all that was.
> I can no more delays devise,
> But welcome pain, let pleasure pass;
> With lullaby now take your leave,
> With lullaby your dreams deceive;
> And when you rise with waking eye,
> Remember then this lullaby.

The movement of the first two lines in triple units reminds us
(though perhaps it is not a conscious intention) how close together lay the symbols of rhetoric and religion; the poem
moves to its slightly heightened conclusion, always plain and
economical, the smaller repetitions, alliterations and plays in
cadence giving the grim recitation its compact, unfaltering
power.

The voice speaking in this poem is distinctive and fully
formed. If it is also limited in scope this is not through any fault
in method or in subject-matter. Gascoigne exploited his talents
and his education to the full, and although it seems likely from
what Gascoigne himself wrote in his *Certayne Notes of Instruction* (1575) that he might have deprecated his own lack of
invention and originality in subject-matter, his efforts at short
poems far exceed his own dreary foray into long poems, *The
Steel Glass*. Many men since Gascoigne have been obsessed with
the idea of the long poem, and have failed to be just to their own
mastery of the short; Keats, for example. Nor is Gascoigne
always as sombre as these two stanzas I have quoted, though he
mostly offers cold comfort. But he can offer it with a rare
pungency, as in *Gascoigne's Memories III*. The aphoristic pithiness
and racy vitality share a good deal with Wyatt's *Second Satire*
which I have glanced at, and both share a lineage going back
beyond Chaucer. This poem describes the morality and the down-
fall of the prodigal; its structure is expository and repetitive,

employing a sort of epigrammatic succession with rapidity and variousness. The repetition, that is, is in the syntax and not the language. The language is mobile and alive. The opening is one of the best things Gascoigne did:

> The common speech is, spend and God will send;
> But what sends he? A bottle and a bag,
> A staff, a wallet, and a woeful end
> For such as list in bravery so to brag.
> Then if thou covet coin enough to spend,
> Learn first to spare thy budget at the brink,
> So shall the bottom be the faster bound;
> But he that list with lavish hand to link
> (In like expense) a penny with a pound,
> May chance at last to sit aside and shrink
> His harebrained head without Dame Dainty's door.
> Hick, Hob, and Dick, with clouts upon their knee,
> Have many times more goonhole groats in store
> And change of crowns more quick at call than he,
> Which let their lease and took their rent before.

It is the tale of the prodigal, hell-bent to destroy his own patrimony, and the figure was an increasing phenomenon in the mid-16th century. Gascoigne hits his characteristic tone, a scornful, truculent resignation which moralises unhesitatingly but is never morose or priggish. That is Gascoigne's most astonishing talent; that he is bluntly didactic without losing the reader. He does most things well in this passage. The rhythm of the second line, for example, is delayed on the question, lifts momentarily on the two syllables of 'and a' and falls like a slap upon 'bag'; after the grand scorn of the opening, the tone shifts to the laconic advice thrown out carelessly,

> 'Learn first to spare thy budget at the brink,'

and the tart contempt of 'shrink/His harebrained head' and so on. Gascoigne shares with Jonson an odd gift for making us read so that each word seems, as it were, to isolate itself for special attention. In Sidney, the words are part of a fluid medium, the line, or more often the whole sentence. In Gascoigne, the peculiar stress on the language gives every word unusual weight. Since Gascoigne follows his own precepts (see p. 24) and writes plainly and in monosyllables, the effect of his poetry, although that effect is got as a result of a good deal of artistry, is of a brusquerie, a succinct outspokenness, a forthright moral certainty and homeliness. Herbert and Donne have been praised for innovating some of these things, but Gascoigne expressed them first, and he could at times bring them to a masterful concentration, as in the central lines of this poem.

> Yet he that yerks old angels out apace
> And hath no new to purchase dignity,
> When orders fall, may chance to lack his grace;
> For haggard hawks mislike an empty hand.
> So stiffly some stick to the mercer's stall,
> Till suits of silk have sweat out all their land;
> So oft thy neighbours banquet in thy hall,
> Till Davie Debit in thy parlour stand
> And bids thee welcome to thine own decay.

The individuality of this comes out if you read it with Jonson's lovely poem *To Penshurst* (see p. 153). Jonson's is a tribute to the noblest way of life he knows; Gascoigne's poem is the final statement of his disenchantment with the economic behaviour of his time, and his state of mind is indicated by his painful sense of loss and of what economic dignity might have been. Instead of this ideal, he affects the philistine posture of bluff good sense, '. . . and then say I/Who speaks the first and keeps the last . . .' etc. Otherwise, he tells us, you are devoured by the carrion birds, and he gives us the terrifying Morality figure of Davie the debtor, standing without warning behind your head.

It is a striking poem. Its individuality *realises* the moral absolutes as a matter of personal experience and this realisation is what poetry is about. All of the sequence *Gascoigne's Memories* is worth reading, as are the brief poems *A Strange Passion of a Lover*, *The Lullaby of a Lover* (considered already), the very impressive *De Profundis*, and a good deal of the fetchingly titled *Dan Bartholomew's Dolorous Discourses* especially the touching last eight lines, which I cannot forbear to quote:

Thus as thou seest I spend both nights and days,
And for I find the world did judge me once
A witless writer of these lovers' lays,
I take my pen and paper for the nonce,
I lay aside this foolish riding rime.
And as my troubled head can bring to pass,
I thus bewray the torments of my time:
Bear with my Muse, it is not as it was.

The last poem I would add to this minimal list is *Gascoigne's Woodmanship*. Elsewhere Gascoigne experiments alongside many contemporaries with the queer metre 'poulter's measure', i.e. regular iambic lines of alternating twelve and fourteen syllables (cf. Southwell's famous poem, *The Burning Babe*), but it is a tyrannic, trotting metre, and nobody made very much of it. The *Woodmanship*, however, is a solid poem and with the third of the *Memories* and the *De Profundis*, probably Gascoigne's best. It displays the virtues I have proposed as peculiarly his: the orderly advance of exposition, the absence of developed imagery, the deliberate measure, the bluntness of tone and diction. The poem also indicates his limitations in the occasional clumsiness of phrasing and obtrusive alliteration, but it is marked by a new note of rueful deprecation which softens the familiar and tenacious moralising, the persistent analysis of moral perception, and makes these enterprises fully human. Gascoigne always sounds such a *decent* person, that we may tend to condescend to him and miss the precision and authority of the man. The *Woodmanship* poem appears as a letter of apology to his patron for his, Gascoigne's, incompetence, first as a member of their shooting party; but this failure becomes a metaphor for his failure in his courtly careers as lawyer, student, soldier and man-about-town. These strictures upon himself involve strictures upon a society which demands often pretentious or dishonest antics from its successful members, and so the poem's argument returns to Gascoigne's primary subject—a Christian-stoical rejection of the world presented in a transparent allegory. The concluding section of twenty-four lines repeats and condenses the allegory and the argument, and emphasises its urgency as personal experience:

But since my Muse can to my Lord rehearse
What makes me miss, and why I do not shoot,
Let me imagine in this worthless verse
If right before me, at my standing's foot
There stood a doe, and I should strike her dead,
And then she prove a carrion carcass too,
What figure might I find within my head
To excuse the rage which ruled me so to do?
Some might interpret by plain paraphrase
That lack of skill or fortune led the chance,
But I must otherwise expound the case;
I say Jehovah did this doe advance
And made her bold to stand before me so,
Till I had thrust mine arrow to her heart,
That by the sudden of her overthrow
I might endeavour to amend my part,
And turn mine eyes that they no more behold
Such guileful marks as seem more than they be:
And though they glister outwardly like gold,
And inwardly but brass, as men may see.
And when I see the milk hang in her teat,
Methinks it saith, 'Old babe, now learn to suck,
Who in thy youth couldst never learn the feat
To hit the whites which live with all good luck'.

(A 'carrion' doe is pregnant and therefore not to be shot at. A 'white' doe is the proper target.)

The painstaking exposition of the moral meaning may seem stodgy and laborious to many modern tastes, but the sobriety, the terseness, the steady and upright carriage of language and feeling seem to deserve a praise infrequently given to such poetry. 'Decency' is not an easy concept to handle, but I think it is needed here. If Gascoigne holds a minor place in literature, yet he is an honourable and moving writer, he contributed essential work to the establishment of an essential style, and we should not slight him for being less engaging than some more shallow men.

NASHE

The most famous poems of Nashe and Ralegh are by contrast immediately commanding, though hardly 'engaging'. Nashe's

In Time of Plague is another poem of valediction to the world, at a time when the epidemic made farewell into an unusually tense and uncertain matter. If one objects that there is a sameness about all these poems which renounce the joys of the world, there are two rejoinders. The first is that many poems which embrace those joys may be much the same as one another, and the interest lies in those who say these things with zest and colour; the second rejoinder depends on the first. The poems of renunciation which survive hold our attention because they embody the necessary strength for their individual survival. *In Time of Plague* is comparable to Ralegh's *Even Such is Time*, but it is not the same poem, nor could it be taken for one of Vaux's. The grave and relentless movement of Nashe's poem is only his; the manner is available for him to use and he uses it, but no one else set down these austere words:

> Beauty is but a flower
> Which wrinkles will devour;
> Brightness falls from the hair;
> Queens have died young and fair;
> Dust hath closed Helen's eyes,

and every stanza closes with the terrible dirge,

> I am sick, I must die—
> Lord, have mercy on us.

Once again, the lines as a unit control the propositions; the haunting images are actual and everyday and they arise from the logic of the poet's thought; the metre is powerful and subdued, varying from regular iambics to an echo of the medieval three-stress line and back again; the language is stern and brief. The poem is flawless, for (as J. V. Cunningham puts it) it 'is the experience of syllogistic thinking with its consequences for feeling, attitude and action. It is a mode of experience that the Renaissance practised and cherished . . . it is a poetical experience and a logical, and it is both at once' (*Tradition and Poetic Structure* p. 58).

Wit with his wantonness
Tasteth death's bitterness;
Hell's executioner
Hath no ears for to hear
What vain art can reply:
I am sick, I must die—
    Lord, have mercy on us.

Haste, therefore, each degree
To welcome destiny;
Heaven is our heritage:
Earth but a player's stage;
Mount we unto the sky;
I am sick, I must die.
    Lord, have mercy on us.

RALEGH

One of Ralegh's most famous poems picks up the metaphor of
life as a part acted on a stage; it is of course a cliché in some
Elizabethan poetry, but Ralegh brings it back to life in a characteristic way:

What is our life? A play of passion,
Our mirth the music of division;
Our mothers' wombs the tiring houses be,
Where we are dressed for this short comedy;
Heaven the judicious sharp spectator is
That sits and marks still who doth act amiss;
Our graves that hide us from the searching sun
Are like drawn curtains when the play is done.
Thus march we playing to our latest rest,
Only we die in earnest, that's no jest.

Once more, this is a poem of renunciation, and again it is worth
worrying about a point I have noted before. What have we to
do with the poetry of death? Such poetry, as it is good, implies a
complementary attitude to life. Because the attitude to death is
what it is, the poet can carry on living well for the present, with
the intelligence and maturity which will in the end permit him to
lay the claims of life aside. The sanctions which in their different

ways, Gascoigne, Nashe and Ralegh see as a part of death, operate as cause and explanation of the best parts of life. And this attitude comes to seem a criterion of humanity to the best minds (and poets) of the 17th century. I have already pointed out how the Christian Humanism of a man like More may communicate itself by an electrical metaphor: the tense, vibrant play in his life and writing between the two poles of renunciation and enjoyment. It is at least arguable that the same tension is apparent in the poetry of many of the great figures between 1500 and 1660. Shakespeare, Jonson, Donne, Herbert, Marvell, all mingle and oppose the irresistible and contradictory forces which pull them towards the sensuous and ascetic lives. Such a tension appears at a high and paradoxical pitch in this and other poems by Ralegh. For the dominant tone here is one of scornful rejection, but the rejection would sedate nobody. The rhythm moves with a nervous angularity which precludes any ease of response. The conventional metaphor ('all the world's a stage') springs to life within the adjectives ('judicious sharp' and 'searching') and the threat of the simple active verbs 'sits and marks'. And extraordinary defiance lurks behind the lines and releases itself in the bitter nonchalance of the last line. The last word of the last sardonic phrase, 'that's no jest', makes a pun which tells us much about Ralegh's habits of mind. 'Jest' means both a joke and a theatrical gesture, and in its throwaway contempt concentrates the grand patrician manner into a word. The Devon chawbacon and adventurer beats the courtiers at their own game. The same tendency finds cruder and more violent expression in the epitaph of the Earl of Leicester (a hazard in studying Ralegh is the difficulty of finding what he wrote. Much was anonymous, much lost, and this is only a probable ascription).

Here lies the noble warrior that never bloodied sword;
Here lies the noble courtier that never kept his word;
Here lies his Excellency that governed all the state;
Here lies the Lord of Leicester that all the world did hate.

The simple savagery of this would have delighted Blake. If the poem is Ralegh's, then it fits what we know of him, and what comes out in the verse. He went his own way, lonely, proud and cryptic, and though he was flashily and fiercely ambitious, he could judge his ambitions as trivial and let his impassioned bitterness destroy in verse all that was now unattainable and for which he had as passionately yearned. Two memorable poems do this: *The Lie* and *Farewell to the Court*. *The Lie* employs in compressed form a sequence of aphorisms which restate a single theme in various aspects and according to Ralegh's notion of the importance of his example. The subject is the contemptible condition of the world, and it is contemplated from a position of haughty and uncontrollable pride. Yet Ralegh gets away with it. The poem renounces and despises all it describes, it relies on a tiny number of grammatical structures, but an astonishing control of minute alterations in cadence and phrasing makes the performance totally commanding. Yet one might praise it with some sense of affront, it is *so* insolent. No one else (not even Shakespeare in *Sonnet 66*) has used the method of repetition with such authority. I think it is the insistent imperative which vindicates it, and makes the renunciation such a dramatic affair. Nothing sullen or sedate here; the feeling proceeds from a sense of headstrong involvement and rancorous disappointment. The renunciation is muted by the insults. I quote two isolated stanzas:

> Tell zeal it wants devotion,
> Tell love it is but lust;
> Tell time it metes but motion,
> Tell flesh it is but dust:
> And wish them not reply,
> For thou must give the lie.
>
> Tell age it daily wasteth;
> Tell honour how it alters;
> Tell beauty how she blasteth;
> Tell favour how it falters:
> And as they shall reply,
> Give every one the lie.

It is not often in Elizabethan (or any other) poetry that time is treated so disparagingly ('it metes but motion') and though the 'lust/dust' rhyme is in every Elizabethan's notebook, there is no one but Herbert in *Church-Monuments* who has used it so awfully as here. The repetition, verbal as well as grammatical, works most memorably in this stanza:

> Tell arts they have no soundness,
> But vary by esteeming;
> Tell schools they want profoundness,
> And stand too much on seeming:
> If arts and schools reply,
> Give arts and schools the lie.

He reduces the imperatives and eases the battering force of the rhyme words by giving them unstressed last syllables, and sets the force elsewhere by repeating 'arts' and 'schools'. Without contrivance, the poem moves to its wry, ambiguous conclusion:

> So when thou hast, as I
> Commanded thee, done blabbing
> (Although to give the lie
> Deserves no less than stabbing)
> Stab at thee he that will,
> No stab the soul can kill.

The body of poems definitely by Ralegh is small, and it is clear that Ralegh was only an intermittent and amateur poet, though a writer of great gifts. He was an extraordinary man. He professed wide interest in the new scientific and alchemical activities; he was widely hated for his exhibitionist arrogance and yet his small circle of intellectual friends was devoted to him; he was a leading monopolist at a time when monopolies were the centre of every economic controversy and when he himself spoke out against them; in all this public endeavour his poetry played a smallish part, and was either a private therapy or a piece of politicking—a means to favour or admiration. The long poem *Ocean's Love to Cynthia* of which only the eleventh book survives was written in fragments to win the Queen's favour. The book which survives was a late addition after Ralegh had been imprisoned and it represents a very skilful and elaborate tribute by way of restoring his fortune. According to the weird conventions of Elizabeth's court, Ralegh pretends in the poem to be hopelessly in love with the Queen, and the poem expounds this. What the poem in fact becomes is an exploration of the courtly ceremony, ambition and scheming to which he has committed himself. It becomes a spiritual trial, and it moves on to a level of charged intellectual exposition where it surpasses most rival attempts in English literature. Now, in fairness to *The Faerie Queene* and to the declared intention of this volume, I must not pursue what is a long fragment very far. Besides, the poem has many rough edges and gaps, and it was clearly unfinished—the Elizabethan criteria of decorum, accentual precision, logic and resonance of imagery, intricate but accurate syntax, correctness of development, would all find the poem wanting. But I shall quote five bold stanzas by way of suggesting what we might have had from Ralegh:

And though strong reason hold before mine eyes
The images and forms of worlds past,
Teaching the cause why all those flames that rise
From forms external, can no longer last,

Then that these seeming beauties hold in prime
Love's ground, his essence and his empiry,
All slaves to age and vassals unto time,
Of which repentance writes the tragedy.

But this, my heart's desire could not conceive
Whose love's outflew the fastest-flying time;
A beauty that can easily deceive
The arrest of years, and creeping age outclimb,

A spring of beauties which time ripeth not,
Time that but works on frail mortality,
A sweetness which woe's wrongs outwipeth not,
Whom love hath chose for his divinity,

A vestal fire that burns, but never wasteth,
That loseth nought by giving light to all,
That endless shines eachwhere and endless lasteth,
Blossoms of pride that can nor fade nor fall.

OCEAN'S LOVE TO CYNTHIA, 173-93

There are disjunctions here, and the writing is rough in one or two places, but mostly this extract can stand beside some of the best in Shakespeare's sonnets. The language is simple and the rhetorical devices small, subdued to the clear definition of the feeling, but the movement of the lines, especially the last two, is radiant and piercing and unimpeachably real. The ancient opposition between reason and passion lives vividly in Ralegh's personal experience. As in so much of Shakespeare, the pressure of time is terrible, but is faced with calm and turned by wit. The second stanza quoted is a grand example of this rare strength, yet the third promptly tips it on its head. It is with such an effort behind him that Ralegh can achieve a poem as upright as *The Passionate Man's Pilgrimage*, or as brief but as consummate as *Even Such is Time*, to which the note is attached on the manuscript, 'These verses following were made by Sir Walter Ralegh the night before he died and left at the Gatehouse.' I do not wish to pump a novelesque significance into Ralegh's value for us; but to fill out the stature of the man behind this small batch of poems, here is an extract from a letter written to his wife just before he was granted an earlier stay of execution. The virtues of this man and this prose are evidenced in his few poems, and they are not narrow.

When I am gone, no doubt you shall be sought by many; for the world thinks, that I was very rich. But take heed of the pretences of men, and their affections; for they last not but in honest, and worthy men; and no greater misery afterwards to be despised: I speak not this (God knows) to dissuade you from marriage, for it will be best for you, both in respect of the world and of God.

As for me, I am no more yours, nor you mine, Death hath cut us asunder; and God hath divided me from the world, and you from me.

Remember your poor Child, for his Father's sake, who chose you, and loved you, in his happiest times.

Get those letters (if it be possible) which I writ to the Lords, wherein I sued for my life. God is my witness, it was for you and yours I desired Life. But it is true that I disdain myself for begging it, for know it (dear wife) that your son is the son of a true man, and one, who in his own respect, despiseth Death, and all his misshapen and ugly shapes.

I cannot write much; God he knows, how hardly I steal this time, while others sleep: and it is also high time, that I should separate my thoughts from the world.

Beg my dead body, which living was denied thee; and either lay it at Sherbourne (if the Land continue) or in Excester Church by my father and mother.

I can say no more, time and death call me away.

The everlasting, powerful, infinite and omnipotent God, that Almighty God who is goodness itself, the true life, and true light, keep thee, and thine, have mercy on me, and teach me to forgive my persecutors and Accusers, and send us to meet in his glorious kingdom.

My dear wife farewell. Bless my poor Boy, Pray for me, and let my good God hold you both in his arms.

Written with the dying hand of sometime thy husband, but now (alas) overthrown
> Wa:Ralegh.

yours that was, but now not my own.

> W:R:

But the last poem does not need buttressing by this splendid letter. It is perfect in itself, it is incomparable.

> Even such is time which takes in trust
> Our youth, our joys, our all we have,
> And pays us but with age and dust;
> Who in the dark and silent grave,
> When we have wandered all our ways,
> Shuts up the story of our days.
> But from this earth, this grave, this dust,
> My God shall raise me up, I trust.

Here the native style touches its height. Rhetoric and logic are in few places so completely a part of the poet's organising genius. The education has become the man. Thus the lines mark off the grammatical units; the logic of argument and syntax order the shape of the experience—'Even such is time which . . . and . . . who . . . when . . . shuts up . . . but . . . my God . . . I trust.' The language is as taut and bare as the logic, further secured by the faintly audible alliterations ('time . . . trust' 'shut . . . story') and the balancing of tripartite phrases in the second and seventh lines. The rhyme scheme completes the patterns, especially in the clinching second use of 'trust' (emphatically not an agnostic irony but a statement of faith). The poem is sombre and final; if it is also static, it is not the stasis of complacent gloom but of conviction won in the teeth of fear and passion. It costs much in human effort to be able to write like this. It is not the only way to write, but it is a good way. Ralegh and the others made it a part of the language; the next chapter looks at the alternative way.

4

Courtesy and Meditation: Edmund Spenser, Sir Philip Sidney and his circle, and Robert Southwell

Spenser is the subject of a complete volume in this series (*Spenser*, Elizabeth Watson) and this chapter makes no attempt to appraise all his short poems which might contribute to the subject of this book. I take him first because he wrote two of the most beautiful poems in English on marriage, because those poems went a good way towards civilising the language, and lastly because they conveniently exemplify what is meant by Petrarchanism and represent its achievement at its most impressive. Petrarchanism is an elaboration, after the decisive intervention of one poet, of a medieval code of chivalry, and of the extension of amorous metaphors into ethical and religious behaviour. Medieval chivalry, like all medieval patterns of living, is strongly allegorical and metaphorical, and this mingling of divine and human love, of chivalry and allegory is the main principle of Spenser's *Faerie Queene*. That poem therefore can be seen as the largest product of Petrarchan attitudes in English literature, but it is irrelevant to our main concerns here because it is an epic. It is committed to a long, wavy narrative line which poses special (and to my mind, ruinous) problems to the poet, and which the writer of the short poem deliberately avoids. *The Faerie Queene* is a monument to Renaissance eloquence and rhetorical virtuosity, but we may study the same, often beautiful qualities more briefly in his two short poems, *Prothalamion* and *Epithalamion* (the words denote celebratory marriage songs, one before and one after the ceremony; this was an acknowledged poetic ritual at the time, finely used by Donne). The second poem is attached to a sequence of sonnets called *Amoretti* and the whole thing was published lateish in Spenser's career, in 1595 when Spenser was forty-three, successful and well known. It is understandably conjectured that the volume describes his own courtship and marriage, but what is important is that in spite of conventionally Petrarchan (and human) disappointments, frustrations, hopes and darkness throughout the love affair, the relationship is not just a ritual piece of Courtly Love, nor is it the doomed and clandestine passion of two married lovers, like Sidney's *Astrophel and Stella*. The affair, and the sequence, proceeds to marriage, and solid domestic satisfactions are its end. It is remarkable that there are few such poems in English literature, and this is a sad lack. These poems deserve to stand beside the most beautiful parts of *The Tempest* and *The Winter's Tale* which rejoice at a particular marriage, and by implication rejoice also at the human potentiality which marriage creates.

The *Prothalamion* is a set of ten eighteen-line stanzas which describe a light and stylised action in order to provide occasions for elaborate decoration. The poet stands by the River Thames, itself an emblem of continuity and fertile peace, watches a crowd of nymphs pay ritual homage with flower-petals (cf. confetti) to a pair of swans, while one sings them a song presaging happiness. The swans process to London, mention of which gives Spenser prompting for a brief aside on the disappointments of his career, but which is more properly the site of the marriage of the swans, now become maidens, to two handsome knights, esquires to the Earl of Essex (Elizabeth's favourite) who is duly acclaimed. Each verse ends with the famous and haunting refrain, picked up by Eliot for ironic use in *The Waste Land*:

'Sweet Thames! run softly till I end my song.'

But I quote a whole stanza:

Then forth they all out of their baskets drew
Great store of flowers, the honour of the field,
That to the sense did fragrant odours yield,

All which upon those goodly birds they threw
And all the waves did strew,
That like old Peneus' waters they did seem
When down along by pleasant Tempë's shore,
Scattered with flowers, through Thessaly they stream,
That they appear, through lilies' plenteous store,
Like a bride's chamber floor.
Two of these nymphs meanwhile two garlands bound
Of freshest flowers which in that mead they found,
The which presenting all in trim array,
Their snowy foreheads therewithal they crowned,
Whilst one did sing this lay
Prepared against that day,
Against their bridal day, which was not long:
Sweet Thames! run softly, till I end my song.

This is the eloquent style. It is the style of erotic sentiment, and it has led to fine things. It becomes the inheritance of Keats in *Endymion* and *Ode to a Nightingale*, of Tennyson in *Ulysses*, and of the modern American, Wallace Stevens, almost anywhere. Spenser's stanza is gently varied in its rhythm, its movement is liquid and its pictorial images opulent. The poet uses heavily stylised language—'snowy foreheads', 'nymphs', 'garlands', all the imagery of the mythological paradise Arcadia where it is always sun-drenched, fresh midsummer. The idea is not to give us a 'realistic' picture, but to arrange the stylised properties in a formal and beautiful dance. Spenser revives Arcadia by the touches of graceful movement, by the lush, sensuous ornaments, 'fragrant', 'plenteous', the heaps of flowers, and by the plaintive charm of his refrain.

The better-known *Epithalamion* is also a stronger poem. It has twenty-three stanzas, also of eighteen lines each, and a short concluding envoi. Each stanza is punctuated by a short line at regular intervals, and possesses a loosely regulated rhyme scheme of which this is a fair example: *ababccdcdeefggffhh*. The poem is a single paean of praise to his lady, presented as an elaborate song whose only principle of order is the stages of his lady's marriage. In so long a poem, this principle is not always enough, and often becomes diffuse, but the lofty rhetoric, the high eloquence and lavish ornament are almost always splendid and moving, and if the poem lacks concentration, the subject is important and glad enough to hold the poem up. And to Spenser, the subject is more than just a lady, or even marriage to a lady, though these would be considerable themes in themselves. For the Renaissance, and especially its garrulous spokesman Petrarch, had urged the study of Plato on Western Europe, and a new platonism was woven densely into the stuff of 16th-century English thought. Plato's famous image for the intellectual aspirations of men, that they perceive only the shadows cast by Ideal Forms upon a darkened wall, persistently tantalised the Elizabethans. To the Protestant mind, it was a duty to search out amongst those wavering and obscure outlines the definite proportions of that Ideal which at once contained the shapes of the Platonic trinity, Beauty, Truth and Goodness. To the literary sensibility trained on Petrarch and Tasso the physical beauty of the mistress became an emblem of her moral and intellectual beauty, and this in turn was a version of Ideal Beauty. Since Ideal Beauty was in part synonymous with truth, the beauty of the mistress became a guide to moral perfection and therefore a proper subject for worship. This neo-Platonic attitude is intimately a part of all the sonnet-sequences and most of the love poems of the time, and it hovers behind a good deal of religious verse. It is particularly strong in Sidney: indeed, it is his subject.

Epithalamion opens in an approved manner with an appeal to the Muses to advance the poet's art, an appeal which sets the 'sugared' style of the poem (the term is Elizabethan). Therefore the substance of the poem is largely descriptive, and its details comfortably transcend the usual Petrarchan wardrobe and take on a life of their own. They are fresh, eager and lovely.

> And let them also with them bring in hand
> Another gay garland
> For my fair love, of lilies and of roses,
> Bound truelove-wise with a blue silk riband.
> And let them make great store of bridal posies,
> And let them eke bring store of other flowers
> To deck the bridal bowers.

And let the ground whereas her foot shall tread,
For fear the stones her tender foot should wrong,
Be strewed with fragrant flowers all along,
And diapered like the discoloured mead.

The Arcadian idiom is a long way from our taste now, and it was
always (no doubt) a festive way to write, but festivity is a necessary quality, and sensuous ornament gives us a lot of pleasure;
and if we cannot read *Epithalamion* gratefully, then our ears are
stopped to a delightful music, to the delicate and ironic movement of (say) a Campion whose verse uses the Arcadian language
for saying serious things, or to most of the English madrigals,
score and verse alike. Spenser has an ear for such music, and its
strong concord:

And let the roaring organs loudly play
The praises of the Lord in lively notes,
The whiles with hollow throats
The choristers the joyous anthem sing,
That all the woods may answer, and their echo ring.

One may note here, as in my first quotation, a metrical smooth-
ness which conceals redundancy of language and some mechanical construction. This is the inevitable fault of a poem with no
argument apart from the poet's feeling of personal enjoyment—
a feeling which the poet can only express by thickening the
decoration. It is bound to become diffuse and chancy, for the
poet lights upon whatever appeals to him or calls out a stage set
from the Petrarchan collections. Thus he gives us a description
of the sun moving through the heavens to rest, a charming and
fanciful description of his lady in bed, the relevant Arcadian
anecdote is added, and he ends with a rhetorical appeal ('apos-
trophe') to the moon-goddess to encourage fertility on this
wedding night. In every case, allowing for a certain wordiness
and facility in the writing, Spenser's poem is graceful and
fetching, and hits off exactly the correct 'courtesy' he wants. At
its most Petrarchan, the poem is also real and vivid.

Tell me, ye merchants' daughters, did ye see
So fair a creature in your town before,
So sweet, so lovely, and so mild as she,

> Adorned with beauty's grace and virtue's store?
> Her goodly eyes like sapphires shining bright,
> Her forehead ivory white,
> Her cheeks like apples which the sun hath ruddied,
> Her lips like cherries charming men to bite,
> Her breast like to a bowl of cream uncrudded,
> Her paps like lilies budded . . .

In the best Petrarchan way, the lady is 'virtue's store', and every one of the succeeding similes is a Petrarchan cliché, sometimes just cliché ('forehead ivory white'), sometimes touched to life ('cherries charming men to bite' 'uncrudded' 'paps . . . budded'. This is the manner against which Shakespeare wrote his brutal *Sonnet 130*, and it was variously abused, but it is handled here with a softness equalled only by Jonson in the song to Charis (p. 140). And the gentle fancy can modulate into something stately:

> Open the temple gates unto my love,
> Open them wide that she may enter in,
> And all the posts adorn as doth behove,
> And all the pillars deck with garlands trim . . .

The poem ends with a good deal of dignity, appealing to Juno for solid, lasting wedlock and for 'fruitful progeny'. There is no inherent reason why the poem should end where it does, except that the poet has had enough of it, and stops. But mostly he sustains the sugared style with few lapses, the poem has moments of ornate splendour and a lot of lovely detail and offers a worthy example of the English Petrarchan at his best. What the poem lacks, what I find Spenser always lacks, is the moral clarity and intellectual energy of the greater Elizabethans. It is not fair in suggesting such a judgment to limit the argument to these short poems of Spenser's, but I think that the same argument can apply to *The Faerie Queene*. He does not lack moral purpose, for he was a serious man and a Protestant, but he does lack incisiveness and energy. So his poetry tends to become shapeless, ambling towards no special end, and his sensuous gift turns into a cumbrous allegory. He has the graces, but not the necessary toughness. Sir Philip Sidney also had the graces—it is the most famous thing about him; it is now time to see what went with them.

It would be impossible to give a brief life-story of every poet mentioned in these pages, but Wyatt as being the first earned a brief biography, Jonson as being, with Shakespeare, the greatest figure we look at takes another, and Sidney, both because of his legendary status and his unique contribution to the literary climate, deserves his biography here.

The story of his death in 1586 (aged thirty-two) at the Battle of Zutphen during the intermittent Netherland wars is now a fragment of English mythology, alongside Drake's game of bowls and Nelson's blind eye. But Sidney was an Elizabethan legend almost as soon as he died. After his death, the Court staged a solemn ritual at which Sidney's favourite black charger equipped with full ceremonial dress was paraded before the mourners. But it was not as a soldier that many of his contemporaries valued him; on his death a couple of them wrote sharply regretting that he had been allowed to pursue the barbarous work of soldiery, and expose himself to dangers better suited to stupid men. For his intellectual contemporaries Sidney was a patron, a cosmopolitan critic and teacher, and an experimental writer. And he was an inspiration, a model of goodness and grace. Fulke Greville, probably a finer poet than Sidney, none the less deferred to him as the more brilliant and attractive intellectual leader. He knew Sidney from the age of ten when they met as children at Shrewsbury School.

> Though I lived with him and knew him from a child, yet I never knew him other than a man: with such staidness of mind, lovely and familiar gravity, as carried grace, and reverence above greater years. His talk ever of knowledge, and his very play tending to enrich his mind: so as even his teachers found something in him to observe and learn . . .
>
> THE LIFE OF THE RENOWNED SIR PHILIP SIDNEY

The Italian Baldassare Castiglione's classic handbook *The Courtier* was translated into English, significantly enough, in mid-century. The volume marked out a full and exact description of the Renaissance gentleman—his proper accomplishments as poet, musician, sportsman, conversationalist, lover, soldier, and man of affairs.

The influence of this book, which proceeds in a novelesque manner with a series of discussions, was huge; it is clear from all kinds of records that Sidney became the living epitome of Castliglione's ideal, and that his example and presence gave a new force and conviction to the aspirations of Elizabethan intellectuals to make their civilisation comparable in greatness to ancient and modern Italy.

Sidney chose a remarkable and rich education. Though in summary it might look like every bright young man's Grand Tour, it is clear from a host of reports that he brought to his studies an astonishingly quick, responsive and original intelligence. After Shrewsbury School, he went to Christ Church, Oxford, at a time when Camden, Hakluyt the adventurer and journalist, Walter Ralegh, and the political philosopher Richard Hooker were all undergraduates, and it is notable that Sidney's career took him as much among scholars and thinkers as it did among poets. After Oxford he was briefly at Cambridge with Fulke Greville, and then, in the company of a professional diplomat, set out for Europe. He was away, off and on, for five years, and although only twenty-two when he returned, he seemed to have charmed and won by that age a crowd of Europe's most impressive scholars, courtiers and politicians. He learned to speak and read closely in French, Dutch and Italian and, more important, he learned (as Wyatt did, but Sidney more comprehensively) to inherit the European traditions, to transmute the civilisation of old Europe into a new source of moral wealth. Sidney's most lasting mentor was the international Protestant scholar, Hubert Languet, but he studied and was welcomed in Strasbourg, Vienna, the great Dutch university at Leiden, and in the stirring cities of Venice and Padua. All the intellectual influences strongest in Sidney's life were Protestant —Leiden was a great Protestant redoubt, Venice and Padua the freest and most tolerant Italian cities—and his brief view of the appalling massacre of Protestants in Paris confirmed him in his loathing for Catholicism and his admiration for the bleak logic of the Calvinist doctrines (see p. 105). Veronese painted Sidney's portrait in Venice, and by the time he returned to England for the first time after a three-year tour, he was sufficiently famous

Wootton Lodge: exterior—the plain, native style in Elizabethan architecture

Wollaton: the hall—the eloquent and magnificent style

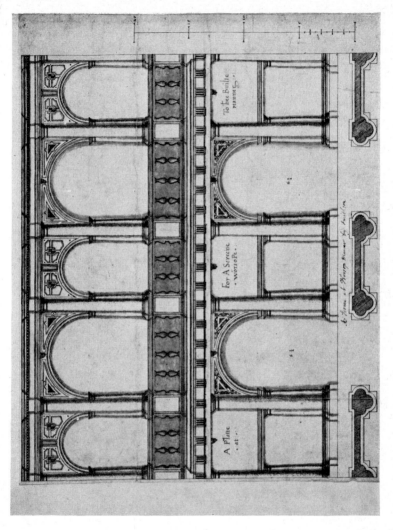

To bee Buillde manner...

For A Screene worsoPe...

A Platte ...at...

Design for a screen at Worksop Manor—structure and proportions in Elizabethan architecture

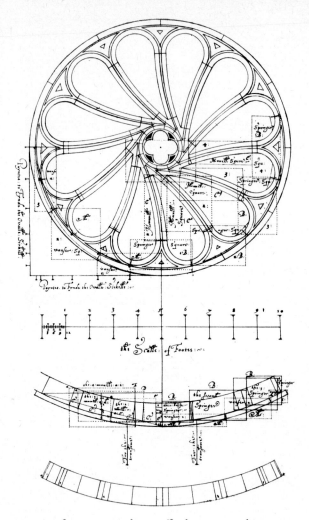

Drawing for a rose window—effortless grace and intensity

and winning for the Queen to send him back on diplomatic missions. He had built for himself a European reputation and acquired an education which fitted him uniquely as a patron, a critic and a poet. The trouble may turn out to be that posterity has given Sidney more attention than even his magnetic personality and striking talent deserve, and allowed his kind of poetry to obscure another.

Some time after about 1577, Wilton House became one of the literary centres of England. Sidney's sister Mary married the Earl of Pembroke and Wilton was their home. We cannot say how many poets (soldiers, politicians, thinkers, musicians and so on) gathered there at any time until Mary's death in 1621, but we may take the place as a model of the best a literary 'court' could do. And there is no doubt that Sidney himself, his sister Mary, Fulke Greville, and a number of lesser but honest writers such as Samuel Daniel, Edward Dyer and the shadowy figure hidden behind the initials 'E. K.' met there regularly. Spenser was often a visitor, and probably the greatest of English musicians, William Byrd, came also. Each of the men experimented freely with new forms and hypotheses. They tried out classical metres in English, they wrote dozens of songs for setting to music, they tried their hand at intimate drama, and they all attempted a full-scale sonnet sequence. Sidney was the most daring experimenter, and his prose romance studded with poems, *Arcadia*, though now a bulky and dusty monument, is the product of an audacious and original intelligence. Nowadays it is probably unreadable except for scholarly reasons, but it is often gay, intellectually vivacious and intent, and always individual. The difference between Sidney's work and Greville's is that in spite of his inventiveness, Sidney is incomplete and sometimes trivial. But perhaps this synopsis suggests Sidney's lead in the artistic vanguard of the time. His work is the product of a richly educated intelligence and a marvellous courtesy, and of a man committed to the nourishment and cultivation of a national literature. Greville's is the noblest tribute, from his *Life of Sidney*:

> ... it will be confessed by all men, that this one man's example, and personal respect, did not only encourage learning and honour in

the schools, but brought the affection, and true use thereof into the Court, and Camp. Nay more, even many gentlemen excellently learned amongst us will not deny but that they effected to row, and steer their course in his wake.

But though no literature can survive without replenishment and innovation, novelty does not ensure value. It is judgments as to value that count.

Astrophel and Stella was published some time after Sidney's death and without any authority in 1591; Fulke Greville supervised the full and proper text in 1598. It is certain that much of the text was well known some time before Sidney's death, not only by the immediate Wilton circle, but in manuscript to a much wider sample of literate readers in Court cliques. The work is a sequence of 108 sonnets, sprinkled with eleven lyrics, and describes the progress of an uncompleted and, so far as we can tell, unconsummated love-affair. To a large extent, the attitudes of the lover, Astrophel (i.e. 'stargazer'), are familiarly Petrarchan, but on several occasions Sidney writes piercingly of the pressures of a normally urgent love-affair with a married woman. It is always clear that his sense of courtly honour and his strong Protestant conscience revolt against the affair, and his Petrarchan gallantry tenses itself against his sense of decency, and both against his physical desire. But to talk like this poses yet again the problem of the poet's 'sincerity', and to what extent our interest in these poems springs from a salacious urge to know the far end of a bit of gossip, and what comes from a concern for poetry. There was a real Stella (i.e. 'star'): Lady Penelope Rich, five years Sidney's junior, a famous beauty and later a notorious adulteress. But the interest of the sequence is not autobiographical. When it is bad (which is not infrequent) it is bad because the poetry lapses into the banal, stale, or trivial—however 'sincere' Sidney may have felt at the time. What we are looking for and responding to are those poems which are alive because they are good, and good because Sidney has made real (i.e. *realised*) in the vitality of his language and its movement certain qualities, judgments, attitudes to experience. Then we sort amongst these, and decide which seem to us enduring and which frivolous; the art should tell us what was fine in the man, what personal qualities, that is, transcend the particular moment and stand as affirmative witness to life. What I am saying is true no doubt of all poetry, but the reminder is timely when we may become so involved in the Sidney legend as to lose sight of the poetry's successes—as we may in worrying about the homosexuality Shakespeare may be writing of in the *Sonnets*. The test, then, is of a poem's reality, its precise, vivid realisation in terms of thought and feeling, and this test applies as surely to a piece of Elizabethan showmanship as it does to a 'sincere' poem. A poem may be slight, a tissue of elaborate tricks and contrivances, but none the less a finer, more realistic poem than a 'sincere' confession. This is a famous example:

> With how sad steps, O Moon, thou climb'st the skies!
> How silently, and with how wan a face!
> What! may it be that even in heavenly place
> That busy archer his sharp arrows tries?
> Sure, if that long-with-love-acquainted eyes
> Can judge of love, thou feel'st a lover's case:
> I read it in thy looks: thy languished grace,
> To me that feel the like, thy state descries.
> Then even of fellowship, O Moon, tell me,
> Is constant love deemed there but want of wit?
> Are beauties there as proud as here they be?
> Do they above love to be loved, and yet
> Those lovers scorn whom that love doth possess?
> Do they call virtue there ungratefulness?

ASTROPHEL AND STELLA, 31

It is a gay poem, and a light one. But for all that, it answers, in Hopkins's words, 'a kind of touchstone of the highest or most living art [which] is seriousness, not gravity but the being in earnest with your subject—reality'. The first two lines curve along a slow, languid arc, softened by the sibilants and long vowels. The lazy grace is played off against the affected surprise of 'What!' and the suddenness of 'busy' and 'sharp'. The subdued drama continues in the knowing use of 'sure', the playful affectation of discovery, 'I read it in thy looks', and of inquisitiveness, 'tell me'. The wholly conventional game of mistresses' pride

75

and scorn comes to life in the bones of Sidney's consummate gentleness, in the earnest pretence of the question on which the poem is left open. The poem is a charming trifle; it sports not so much with the lady as with the Petrarchan game, and yet because it so meticulously orders its courtly graces and so completely knows its place, it is a stronger thing than we might first think. The flippancy is perfectly weighed and therefore implies a poised and civilised mind. There are many such poems in the sequence, and this is one of the best of them; you may, perhaps, have too much of this kind of good thing.

It would be impossible to review all the sonnets in the sequence which deserve our attention, and which evidence the qualities of mind and spirit that have made Sidney's name known to those who will never read a line of poetry. The interested reader might begin with numbers *28, 39, 41, 47, 71* (in which Petrarchan elegance is ousted by the unforgettable last line, 'But ah, Desire still cries, "Give me some food!"'), *74, 90,* and *99,* which is especially graceful. This is a brief list, but there is a good deal here to take seriously. Sidney attained an unusual sophistication of technique, expert and unobtrusive in the elegant control of rhythm and language, subduing the mechanism to the decorum of his manners. He rarely exposes the working of a poem for our admiration, though he delights in punning antitheses and tricks of argument. At the end of *47* for example, the urgencies of the voice are gently contained within the pentameter:

> Let her go! Soft, but here she comes! Go to,
> Unkind, I love you not! O me, that eye
> Doth make my heart to give my tongue the lie!

Yet we may feel that Sidney is still playing a game, at least partially, and object that the easy poise comes from having only mild disturbances to set in order. A poet may acquire elegance to conceal the fact that he has no experience to write about. An unattached sonnet, sometimes printed as *110* in *Astrophel and Stella*, refutes this view. Whether or not it formally belongs to the sequence doesn't matter: the poem rejects even the richest human love, and reaffirms in personal accents an ancient Christian attitude:

Leave me, O love, which reachest but to dust,
And thou my mind, aspire to higher things.
Grow rich in that which never taketh rust:
Whatever fades but fading pleasure brings.
Draw in thy beams, and humble all thy might
To that sweet yoke where lasting freedoms be;
Which breaks the clouds and opens forth the light
That doth both shine and give us sight to see.
O take fast hold; let that light be thy guide
In this small course which birth draws out to death,
And think how evil becometh him to slide
Who seeketh heaven and comes of heavenly breath.
Then farewell, world! Thy uttermost I see:
Eternal love, maintain thy life in me.

This, along with one or two of his songs, marks Sidney at his best, and if we feel that in spite of the undoubted distinction of this poem there still is a sense of frailty, an absence of bone and sinew when compared with Greville's 'When all this All' (p. 108), then that feeling may justly place Sidney amongst our value-judgments. His vision is not large. Yet few poets can have handled the sonnet form more nicely. The sonnet, though we take it for granted, is a queer thing. Wyatt fetched it from Italy, but it rapidly became as familiar and necessary a mode to Elizabethan poets as the lyric. There is no place here to analyse its properties at length—some of them, such as the fourteen lines, are completely arbitrary—but we should insist on its essential logic, and the way in which the various rhyme schemes can enforce that logic. Thus the *abba abba* rhyme scheme for the octet ought to emphasise a different kind of logical pattern from that of a sonnet beginning *abab cdcd*; the second kind, which will proceed to a third quatrain *efef*, should be more discursive than the tighter logical relations implied by *abba abba cde cde*. Of course, this is not necessarily so; the close pattern can be used for decorative purposes, and the discursive one (which Shakespeare uses exclusively and is known as 'Shakespearean') dominates the later work. Here, Sidney uses the 'Shakespearean' sonnet in a poem of remarkable beauty and seriousness. It has not the profundity of George

Herbert, but it shows most of his other qualities: the gentleness, the alertness of rhythm and perfection of tone—a serious courtesy, the voice dignified and humane. The movement is expert: the first two lines each draw exactly the same stress-contour, but the first treads down 'to dust' and the second lifts on the open syllables of 'higher things'. The cliché device of repetition 'fades . . . fading' revives in the delicate cadence of line four; the paradox of line six does not decorate, but *realises* its meaning, so that the paradox discovers a moral truth which confirms itself in the gradual radiance of the two verbs 'breaks' and 'opens forth' and their clinching eighth line. The sestet opens with the subdued drama in the four stresses of 'O take fast hold', and goes on to extend and seal the renunciation. The poem is faultlessly symmetrical and articulated, the rhythmic shifts are precise yet very slight, so that we need to listen hard to take their point; the complete consort of the poem is fluent and magnificent. And when we set beside this poem, songs such as *Who Hath His Fancy Pleased; Who Is It That This Dark Night*, and *Only Joy, Now Here You Are* with its heartbreaking refrain, the tender altercation between lover and lady:

> Take me to thee, and thee to me.
> 'No, no; no, no, my dear, let be.'

Sidney can stand sturdily at the feet of the giants.

The second of these songs must be among the finest love songs in English; it surpasses anything like it even in Hardy, and in part it surpasses its own subject and treatment as it records the argument between lover and lady about the pressures on their love from time, from their own reason, and from other people's gossip. One verse will make clear how far Sidney moves beyond Petrarchan fancies and turns the opposition of reason and passion into the most caressing compliment.

> 'But your reason's purest light
> Bids you leave such minds to nourish'.
> Dear, do reason no such spite;
> Never doth thy beauty flourish
> More than in my reason's sight.

Sidney uses dramatised conversations in his poetry as much as any of the 17th-century masters, but though he is less dazzling than Donne and less profound than Herbert, his conversation is unfailingly sweet and gentle, capable of humour and irony, distinct, clear and completely enchanting. These are rare virtues, and we can hardly do without them. Sidney takes his place in the making of a conversation whose various accents come from Wyatt, Ben Jonson, and the song-writers. These are very different men, but they speak together; they founded a way of speech, and it is a good way. Sidney himself in his *Apologie for Poetrie* (written about 1580) best describes his own poetry and writes a programme for English poetry:

> He [the poet] beginneth not with obscure definitions, which must blur the margin with interpretations, and load the memory with doubtfulness; but he cometh to you with words set in delightful proportion, either accompanied with, or prepared for the well-enchanting skill of music.

Sidney's translation of the Psalms is a neglected and uneven piece of work. He died after completing numbers 1–43, and his remarkable sister the Countess of Pembroke finished them. The Psalms, as we saw in Wyatt, were not an unusual source for poetry, and although there is plenty that is clumsy or primitive in the Sidneys' work, there is also a steady application, so far unseen except in Wyatt, to the poetry of religious meditation, and to combining the versatility and resourcefulness of songs with religious subjects. On the whole, the resulting poetry is of more historical than poetical interest: the poems look forward to the triumph which George Herbert won in *The Temple*; all the same there are some striking stanzas and many strong lines. Yet they lack Sidney's habitual ease of movement (and his sister was less polished than he) for he seemed to be tussling with recalcitrant subjects; but he exhibits an unusual thrust and mobility of ryhthm, and experiments with startling imagery. Along with the awkwardness, there is a fine relish for the blood of the language. One of the best is the sonnet version of *Psalm 150*, where the familiar form gives the Countess confidence. The poem shows much that is best in Elizabethan poetry. It is explicitly musical, it is plain but muscular and decisive, it is grand but decorous. The movements and the statements adjust to one another, enforce and define one another so that the final effect is like the best brass music of the time: strongly chorded (listen to the bold pause enforced after 'conclude' in line 13), discreet, shapely, and joyous. Since the poem is a single *Laudate*, and no more, it does not have the argumentative structure of more complex religious poems. But it speaks with an individual voice on behalf of a whole community, reaching out from a private manuscript to the life of a people.

> O laud the Lord, the God of hosts commend,
> Exalt his power, advance his holiness:
> With all your might lift his almightiness:
> Your greatest praise upon his greatness spend.
>
> Make trumpet's noise in shrillest notes ascend:
> Make lute and lyre his lovéd fame express:
> Him let the pipe, him let the tabret bless,
> Him organ's breath, that winds or waters lend.
>
> Let ringing timbralls so his honour sound,
> Let sounding cymbals so his glory ring
> That in their tunes such melody be found,
> As fits the pomp of most triumphant king.
> Conclude: by all that air, or life enfold,
> Let high Jehovah highly be extolled.

ROBERT SOUTHWELL

Robert Southwell helped to settle certain of the qualities of the great English style, and he made some novel suggestions. He wrote very few good poems, but he relocated and deepened the growing tradition. The qualities he recommends, in spite of his militant Catholic evangelism, sound at times remarkably like Gascoigne's. Moral and literary descriptions are scarcely separable, so when in his simple primer *A Short Rule of Good Life* (1598?) Southwell urges certain behaviour on his readers, it is not hard to transfer the ruling to poetry. He asks for 'external decency', for 'decent and comely' dress, 'handsome and clean, and as much as may be without singularity, that therein the staidness and seemly estate of my soul may be perceived'. He is gay, 'rather bent to smiling, than heaviness, and free from frowning, and such like unseemly distemper'; and he keeps good house: 'go about the rooms . . . and see that they be kept clean and handsome, thinking that God is delighted in cleanliness, both bodily and ghostly, and detesteth sluttishness'. And honest homily of this kind sorts well with this verse, from *Times Go By Turns*:

The sea of fortune doth not ever flow,
She draws her favours to the lowest ebb;
Her tide hath equal times to come and go,
Her loom doth weave the fine and coarsest web;
No joy so great but runneth to an end,
No hap so hard but may in time amend.

There is something of Gascoigne's manner in this, though the bluntness of this is more comfortable than his, and without the same pitch of feeling. But, as we have seen, gnomic (or proverbial) verse, stiffened by the alliterative habit, had a good run, made for a few very fine poems, and was a better model for a tyro than Petrarchan verse. Though Southwell managed some goodish small poems in this manner, he did not possess a sufficiently austere and aloof personality to carry it off like Ralegh. On such poems, he does not really command a place in this review. But Southwell did something else. He brought to England the texts and disciplines of the Counter-Reformation, with its devotional manners and its art of meditation. The Catholic evangelists initiated through the 16th-century saints a technique of prayer and meditation with very specific rules and procedures, and an exhausting programme of execution. Southwell, a recusant Catholic, learned these methods from the Jesuits in Rome and returned afire to England intent upon subversion (he was betrayed after six years' work in 1592, and publicly executed after severe torture). He brought together the meditative techniques he had learned with the language of Petrarchan verse, the jauntiness and gaiety of the love lyrics, their versatile stanza-forms. And he made this, *Mary Magdalen's Complaint at Christ's Death*:

Since my life from life is parted:
Death come take thy portion;

Who survives, when life is murdered,
  Lives by mere extortion.
All that live, and not in God,
Couch their life in death's abode.

This is deft and light. It takes the airiest gestures from the songs and relates them to a religious feeling, and in doing this helps to fuse the native and the Petrarchan styles and to make the great works possible. A study of the art of meditation is as much a part of understanding this poetry, and that of the next century, as is some grasp on the training of the *trivium*; indeed, the two go together, the stages and minuteness of meditation being shaped to the formal patterns of logic and rhetoric. Meditation regulated and drilled a thinker (and a poet) in the living process of self-analysis; it described how to begin with analysis, proceeding to self-address and ending in colloquy with God; it directed the soul from the intellect to the passions to communion with God. It was relentlessly tripartite in its strictures, echoing religious imagery (especially the Trinity) in its syntax and consequently in its rhyme-schemes and stanza-forms. It is certain that Southwell practised the art, and certain that Donne and Herbert were skilled in it; it is likely that the art affected most of the poets after about 1580, including non-Catholics.

The poets considered in this chapter were busy in the refinement of the language. They were learning to absorb and relocate a welter of past and foreign literature for their own use. They learned to fill certain absences in the English poetic sensibility. Sidney and Spenser are two of the greatest stylists in our literature, though Sidney is probably the more polished as well as being an inveterate experimentalist, and Southwell learned and handed on more European lessons. What Sidney and his circle lacked of moral grandeur and sardonic courage when compared with Ralegh, they made up in gaiety, tenderness, politeness, grace, wit, and in Sidney himself something more. Their work and their strengths are of a piece with the English madrigalists, brought to a peak by Campion. It is to these latter men I now turn, and without their virtues we'd be dull, grim fish.

5

Song and Dance: The Madrigalists and Thomas Campion

The origins and connections of song and dance are sunk deep in the history of liturgy and ritual, but it is important to recall that dance probably came first as a rhythmic, formalised expression of feeling, that spontaneously a formalised chant arose from the dance, and that, probably much later, the two became externally co-ordinated by instrumental direction. These connections were always there—they still are, so that we move our bodies to a catchy tune; a few heavy manual tasks still have songs to accompany the rhythms of the work. The connections between song and dance which concern us in the 16th and early 17th centuries were much closer than they are for us. I have sketched out (p. 26) the way in which national speech rhythms and stresses are blood and sinew to the life of music. In untraceable ways, physical gesture and movement live within language, spoken or musical. Now dance grows from the ritual needs of a society, and these needs were for the Elizabethan courtiers largely ceremonial. Thus their dances are the formal expression of the pattern of courtesy, the hierarchies and deference which justify Court life and the conception of Elizabethan politics. In so far as these policies still carried religious sanctions, the dances implied certain beliefs about the relation of men and women, sexually, socially and in religious terms. The point clarifies itself if we make a brief diagram of a country dance occasionally still in action, *Strip the Willow* (country dances copied metropolitan ones). In this simple, boisterous dance, the man dances with his partner down a row of companions, each partner briefly joins hands with each member of the opposite sex before returning to his own, to be replaced by the next pair. Implicit in the dance is a celebration of marriage, social belonging and human continuity. It illustrates the rich range of associations present in dancing, and the way in which it arises directly from a material (it is fair to say, political) context. The gayest and most appealing of all the Elizabethan madrigalists describes the most popular dances in an essay that I shall quote a good deal. The pavan, longest-lived of all Court dances, is, Thomas Morley says, 'a kind of staid music, ordained for grave dancing, and most commonly made of three strains [or sections], whereof every strain is played or sung twice' (*A Plain and Easy Introduction to Practical Music*, 1597). The galliard, which always followed the pavan, Morley describes as 'a lighter and more stirring kind of dancing than the pavan'; and finally (out of many others) a more democratic caper than the first two, 'The Alman . . . a more heavy dance than this (fitly representing the nature of the people, whose name it carrieth) so that no extraordinary motions are used in dancing of it. It is made of strains, sometimes two, sometimes three, and every strain is made by four, but you must mark that the four of the pavan measure is in double proportion to the four of the *Alman* measure . . .'. Given that dance and song forms were more or less synonymous in the secular music of the time, and that so much of the poetry even when not written specifically for music was infinitely settable to music, then again we must pay close attention to these subtle relations. Morley makes clear to us how much musical education mattered to Elizabethans, in this entertaining anecdote:

> . . . But supper being ended, and music books according to the custom being brought to the table, the mistress of the house presented me with a part, earnestly requesting me to sing. But when after many excuses, I protested unfeignedly that I could not, everyone began to wonder. Yea, some whispered to others, demanding how I was brought up . . .

op. cit.

In fact, we acknowledge the interaction of gesture and language when we talk about the movement of a poem being graceful or heavy. In the special case of Elizabethan sonnets, it is illuminating

to recall that ceremony in the sonnet reflected the actual ceremonies of the Court. But songs and their music had more direct
kinds of influence on literary composition. The grim refrain in
Greville's hymn:

> Deprived of human graces and divine,
> Even there appears this saving God of mine—

CAELICA, 99

which is an organic part of the poem's effect, is a device suggested
by musical practice. The refrain, which started out as linguistic-
ally meaningless and only important to the music, was gradually
woven into tight repetitive structures within the poem. The
various forms of this brought over from Italy, such as the
villanelle, aubade or triolet for singing, gradually attained
independent status as poems. They are capable of a packed
intricacy which is much more than clever, and only recently
William Empson has used these forms to render a brooding,
muffled ominousness which no other form would provide:

> Slowly the poison the whole blood stream fills.
> It is not the effort nor the failure tires.
> The waste remains, the waste remains and kills.

MISSING DATES

English poetry could not have reached the heights it did without
assimilating what Sidney learned in Italy. But English music
created its strengths by itself. Taverner (1495–1545) was an
original master, Tye (1500–73) and the early pioneer Dunstable
(?–1453) possessed respectable gifts. By 1590 when the madrigals
and books of airs start to proliferate, Byrd was in his stride, and
the mighty Tallis was dead. Music therefore was further
developed than poetry. The song tradition, as we have seen in
Wyatt, was old and honourable and pretty capacious; the
religious music had already reached soaring heights. None the
less, it is no accident that the finest flowering of English poetry
coincides with its greatest music. The period of Shakespeare and
Ben Jonson, of the great dramatists and poets, is also the period of
Byrd, Weelkes, Dowland and Gibbons, and it is the period
exactly marked out by the great rush of published songbooks

collected by E. H. Fellowes, *English Madrigal Verse 1588–1632* (1920). The impetus behind the rush came from Italy. While accompanied song was a self-justifying social activity any time after 1450 or so, and the accompaniment was far from primitive, and while this practice replenished itself from a robust tradition of genuine folk-song, the Italian musicians had brought their accompaniments to a much more ornate and brilliant pitch. They had designed the madrigal, very often as a setting for the simplified conventionalities and lush effects of the Petrarchan sonnet. The madrigal decorated and thickened the broad oppositions of the sonnet (i.e. mistress/victim, ice/heat, etc.) with lavish counterpoint or gay, fragile variations. The madrigalists lent delicacy and variousness to what had become slightly threadbare themes, and the English composers learned to bring together vocal inflection and harmonic poignancy. All the same, they were confined to setting fairly simple effects, for when they were not simple, the nature of part-singing obscured the complexity of language and the poem was lost. You cannot hear the words in a madrigal unless they are short, easy and repeated. For the madrigal, Fellowes tells us:

> . . . took the form of unaccompanied song for at least three, and rarely more than six, voice-parts. It was constructed mainly upon short musical phrases treated contrapuntally, while each voice-part had an equal share of melodic interest, the musical phrases being taken up consecutively rather than simultaneously by the various voice-parts, the verbal phrases being several times reiterated. Occasionally this method was varied by short periods in which all the voices moved together in blocks of harmony. The true madrigal was seldom set to more than one stanza of poetry; and indeed these composers studied their words so closely, and expressed themselves with such intimate regard for the particular meaning of each word and each phrase, that the exact repetition of their music to a fresh stanza of words was scarcely ever possible . . . and above all other considerations, they strove to add meaning and point to the words which they had chosen to set.
>
> ENGLISH MADRIGAL VERSE, Preface, pp. ix–x

Byrd finely expressed his purpose in planning 'to frame his music to the life of the word', and Morley bore him out:

We must also have a care so to apply the notes to the words, as in singing there is no barbarism committed; that is, that we cause no syllable which is by nature short be expressed by many notes or one long note, nor no long syllable be expressed with a short note . . . We must also take heed of separating any part of a word from another by a rest, as some dunces have not shacked to do . . . which is one of the greatest absurdities which I have seen committed in the dittying of music.

A PLAIN AND EASY INTRODUCTION, 1597

This is what the madrigalists aimed at. I can't pursue here the relation of words to music in madrigals, but if the reader will take every chance to listen to that famous, very beautiful and much reviled madrigal 'Now is the month of Maying/When merry lads are playing' (which is Morley's) he should hear the elements I have described, and if he doesn't also feel the gaiety and exuberance and sheer physical joy (which comes out particularly in the gleeful nonsense refrain, 'fa la la la la la la') then he is a man of stone, and the truth is not in him. (I suggest some records after the bibliography, p. 167.)

A different sort of madrigal, the Air, was a catchy tune accompanying a poem of several verses and played by a subordinate instrument, generally a lute; and everybody owned a lute. Sometimes the melody would come from exisiting folk-songs, but the composers altered and adorned these and invented numberless ones of their own to gratify a new instinct for musical expressiveness. Morley describes how to set a love poem:

. . . you must possess yourself with an amorous humour (for in no composition shall you prove admirable except you put on and possess yourself wholly with that vein wherein you compose) so that you must in your music be wavering like the wind, sometimes wanton, sometimes drooping, sometime grave and staid, or herewhile effeminate.

op. cit.

The musicians then helped the poets to learn the virtues of playfulness, a magical suggestiveness, fragility of touch, and refinement. They showed (and in this, especially Dowland) how to catch a strange and dreamy melancholy in sound, to haunt a

87

listener by sweet cadences. Remember how often such language occurs in Shakespeare's comedies, early and late.

Lorenzo in *The Merchant of Venice*:

> With sweetest touches pierce your mistress' ear,
> And draw her home with music.

JESSICA: I am never merry when I hear sweet music.

V, *i*, 65–7

The Duke in *Twelfth Night*:

> That old and antique song we heard last night:
> Methought it did relieve my passion much,
> More than light airs . . .

II, *iv*, 3–5

Ariel in *The Tempest*; in fact images of music's occult power pervade Shakespeare.

For the Airs, the composers usually took a single line to fit a musical phrase, as in this lovely melody of Ford's from his *Music of Sundry Kinds*, 1607. It is very simple to play, plaintive and charming.

There is a La-die_ sweet and kind,

was nev – er face so pleasde my mind,

I did but see her pass-ing by And

yet I love her till I die.

2 Her gesture, motion and her smiles,
  Her wit, her voice, my heart beguiles,
  Beguiles my heart, I know not why,
  And yet I love her till I die.

4 Had I her fast betwixt mine arms,
  Judge you that think such sports were harms,
  Were't any harm? no, no, fie, fie,
  For I will love her till I die.

And so on. The poem ends:

6 Cupid is wingéd and doth range,
  Her country so my love doth change,
  But change the earth, or change the sky,
  Yet will I love her till I die.

      AN ELIZABETHAN SONG BOOK, ed. Auden, Kallman, Greenberg

But this, though neat and winning, is too slight for rereading. Morley's setting of this next poem (possibly his own, for he wrote a good many) involves more eloquent music as it is a more resourceful poem. The music indulges the language and commiserates with it. The amused parentheses of the poem betray its playful intent, and the music acts to confirm this irony by keeping a check within its upright phrases, not allowing things to get out of hand. The marriage of words and music is easy, gay and harmonious, each adjusted to the other.

Moderately slow

Faire in a morne oh fair-est morne was
ev - er morne so faire,_____

And on a hill (oh fairest hill, was hill so never blessed)
There stood a man (was never man for no man so distressed)
This man had hap (O happy man, no man so hapt as he)
For none had hapt to see the hap that he had hap to see.

The writer plays with his amused certainty of his own clichés.

As he (behold) this man beheld, he saw so fair a face,
The which would daunt the fairest here, and stain the bravest grace,
Pity, he cried, and pity came, and pitied for his pain,
That dying would not let him die, but gave him life again.

Then he brings things home with a flourish.

For joy whereof he made such mirth, that all the world did ring,
And Pan for all his Nymphs came forth, to hear the shepherds sing,
But such a song song never was, nor ne'er will be again,
Of Phillida the shepherd's Queen, and Coridon the swain.

The poem and the music combine in a lighthearted game, and if
one cannot escape the feeling that the poet is pleased with himself,
why, he has good reason. Stylishness of this kind grows from a
rich civilisation, it rests upon a sure sense of what is serious and
what is flippant, upon standards of taste and propriety. It is consequently more than a private game and as it enchants, so it
refines the ear. Of the composers listed in the Madrigalists'
section of Fellowes's anthology, Byrd, Farnaby, Gibbons,
Morley (who wrote many of his own lyrics), Weelkes and Wil-
bye are probably the best, and among the lutanists or writers of
airs, Campion, John Dowland and (in spite of his tiny output)
John Daniel are the finest. Campion, however, was poet, composer and theoretician of both arts; he was a minute and exqui-
site master of his crafts, and I reserve him for special discussion.
John Dowland was a scarcely lesser artist, an international
lutanist, and a committed melancholic. The reader unfamiliar
with the music of airs and madrigals would best begin with
Dowland's work. It is copious, delightful, often heartbreaking,
always intelligible. He is an amazing virtuoso.

Dear, if you change, I'll never choose again.
Sweet, if you shrink, I'll never think of love.
Fair, if you fail, I'll judge all beauty vain.

> Wise, if too weak, more wits I'll never prove.
> Dear, sweet, fair, wise, change, shrink not; be not weak:
> And, on my faith, my faith shall never break.

This gentle and affectionate stanza, although laden with stresses (the penultimate line is nearly all stress), moves with the springy step a song requires, and the music delicately impresses the difference between the appelatives ('dear', 'sweet', etc.), the conditional clauses ('if you . . .'), the main clauses ('I'll . . .') and the elaborate mixture of threat and compliment in the last couplet. The music is a lesson in how to read the poem. The same is true of the famous song:

> Fine knacks for ladies, cheap, choice, brave and new,

where the stresses are very exactly controlled by the first comma—which throws all the weight on to 'cheap'—and are delayed by the conjunction 'and'. The rest of the poem is as rich an example of the author's technical skill and the way that skill creates and realises the meaning. As in any good poem, the rhythmic control does not merely emphasise or reflect the meaning, it *is* that meaning, the hard, bright definition of thought and feeling at once. 'Fine knacks' is an especially good example, for it elegantly conceals beneath the imitation of a pedlar's song a rueful comment on himself as poet and lover and the relationship between the two:

> Great gifts are guiles, and look for gifts again;
> My trifles come as treasures from my mind.
> It is a precious jewel to be plain.

In the dainty idiom of the song, Dowland (if he is the author) makes his moving statement about his work. George Herbert talks in a very comparable way in *Jordan I* and *II*. The poems in Dowland's three *Books of Airs* (1597, 1600, 1603) and *A Pilgrim's Solace* (1612) are remarkably good, and although he never fails to make the text the centre of the musical act, the music itself is intense and passionate, beautifully responsive even in moments of florid counterpoint to the dramatic mood. A striking example of the quality of his chosen texts is the ninth poem of *A Pilgrim's Solace*, in which the gravity of the valediction is softened by the liquid movement of the pentameter, the good manners of the requests ('Forbear' . . . 'O give me time . . . Or let me die'), the mild wryness at his own posture with which each stanza ends:

> Go, nightly cares, the enemy to rest,
> Forbear awhile to vex my grievéd sprite.
> So long your weight hath lain upon my breast
> That I do live of life bereavéd quite.
> O give me time to draw my weary breath,
> Or let me die, as I desire the death.
> Welcome, sweet Death! O life no life, a hell!
> Then thus and thus I bid the world farewell.
>
> False world, farewell! The enemy to rest,
> Now do thy worst, I do not weigh thy spite;
> Free from thy cares I live for ever blest,
> Enjoying peace, and heavenly true delight,
> Delight whom woes nor sorrows shall amate;
> Nor fears nor tears disturb her happy state.
> And thus I leave thy hopes, thy joys untrue;
> And thus and thus, vain world, again adieu.

But I had not intended to stress a kind of poem in Dowland's settings at which we have already seen Ralegh excel, though this one is gentler and less proud in tone than Ralegh's. Yet it is right that Dowland's settings be first remembered for his characteristic melancholy of tone (his motto was *Dowland semper dolens*), and many from this list are fine examples of these: *If My Complaints Could Passions Move*; *Come, Heavy Sleep*; *If Floods of Tears Could Cleanse My Follies Past*; *Stay, Time, Awhile Thy Flying*. Apart from the songs I should mention Dowland's famous lute piece *Lachrimae* ('tears') which crops up all over Elizabethan music and had a tremendous vogue as well as a real influence. But the last of his settings to consider shows Dowland exploiting the most commonplace of Elizabethan themes, of 'Gather ye rosebuds while ye may' and 'Had we but world enough and time'.

Come a - way, come sweet love, the gold - en morn - ing breaks, Teach thine arms then to em - brace, And sweet___ ros - - ie lips to kisse, And mix our___ soules in mu - tual blisse.

Come away, come, sweet love,
The golden morning wastes,
While the sun from his sphere,
His fiery arrows casts:
Making all the shadows fly,

Playing, staying in the grove,
To entertain the stealth of love.
Thither sweet love let us lie,
Flying, dying, in desire,
Winged with sweet hopes and heavenly fire.

Come away, come, sweet love,
Do not in vain adorn
Beauty's grace that should rise
Like to the naked morn:
Lilies on the river side
And fair Cyprian flowers new blown,
Desire no beauties but their own.
Ornament is nurse of pride,
Pleasure, measure, love's delight;
Haste, then, sweet love, our wishéd flight.

The tender desire of this is allowed to remain candid and complimentary (the references to 'pain' and 'rude disdain' in the first stanza are perfunctory). All the felt delight lies in 'sweet rosy lips', in the buoyancy of the rhythm in its opening lines, and its loitering, caressing motion in the stealthy participles of the second part of each stanza. The music sets out briskly, and then dissolves into lingering rests and cadences. The sexual feeling is joyful without restraint, and avoids the gross or the sentimental. Poetry and music unite in grace, concord, and sensuousness. The capital thus accrued by the partnership of poet and musician was stocked in the reserves of the language.

THOMAS CAMPION

Coming to Campion, we find ourselves aware for the first time throughout the writings of one man, of all the work which has been completed. Wyatt, for example, had a tougher and more tenacious mind, Spenser had greater scope, but in Campion's work we can sense the contemporaneity of Donne, Greville, Shakespeare and Ben Jonson. We do not sense the same consistency in Ralegh because he was busy and probably careless, and his poetry was not for him the central activity it was for the others; but Campion, though unmistakably minor, is riding the

95

accumulated riches of the previous half-century. Those of his books that were published during his lifetime and bear any date are marked 1595 and 1613, and at least two were published between 1613 and his death in 1620. He is therefore writing in the three decades which saw the high point of the short poem, of music, and of dramatic poetry in English literature. The ease and purity he manifests are the fruit of the gradual, diligent cultivation and ripening of the language at the hands of the earlier poets. Although the poetry of any period will include a great deal of rubbish (these thirty years as well) the work of someone as distinguished as Campion speaks eloquently for the intellectual and emotional training and civilisation which made it possible. It is fair to define minor poetry as that composition which engages an aspect (or aspects) of man's experience, which treats that experience fully, but not as a matter of total centrality. A major poem engages, communicates and understands a central experience in its essential and inclusive terms. The minor poem is by definition a more modest affair, but it can constitute a necessary statement about everyday behaviour. It sorts out the less resonant but real and immediate difficulties of familiar relationships and achieves this in a satisfying entirety denied to any but the very greatest writers in a major mode. Goodness me, the delights of everyday pleasures need no justification. We cannot always be posted at the heights of the sublime. The minor poem refreshes the spirit.

> I must complain yet do enjoy my love;
> She is too fair, too rich in lovely parts:
> Thence is my grief, for Nature, while she strove
> With all her graces and divinest arts
>   To form her too too beautiful of hue,
>   She had no leisure left to make her true.

> Should I, aggrieved, then wish she were less fair?
> That were repugnant to mine own desires:
> She is admired, new lovers still repair;
> That kindles daily love's forgetful fires.
>   Rest, jealous thoughts, and thus resolve at last:
>   She hath more beauty than becomes the chaste.

Campion's subject-matter is largely though not exclusively Petrarchan, but he handles the Petrarchan vocabulary with remarkable restraint and lightness. He consummates the union of speech rhythms and metrical elegance, masters the Petrarchan tricks of paradox ('She hath more beauty . . .') and repetition ('love/lovely') and strikes the conventional postures with so dainty and ironic an air that they come gaily to life, recharged with all kinds of implication, sensual, insolent, courteous, mocking. The poem I quote is not trivial, because, as Dr. Leavis finely says in an analogous context, 'that game [the poet plays] we feel also as an exercise in the art of verse; we are aware at the same time of an attitude towards that art, and in that attitude we have the presence of Ben Jonson' (*Revaluation*, p. 41). These strengths are present in this deceptive poem. The first deflates the convention by making it clear how detached Campion can be from the situation (real or imagined). He softens the strenuous words like 'grief' and 'strove' by locating them in these fluent, unbroken rhythms. The 'too, too' is again a mild deflation of customary excesses, the placing of the delightful adjective 'aggrieved' fastidiously mocks his own taste for pretty girls. He stills the faint ruffling of the poem's surface by his judicious 'Rest', and affects to settle what has never been more than a pseudo-problem (since he obviously doesn't want the lady to be chaste) by his pert paradox,

> She hath more beauty than becomes the chaste.

He knows quite well that this is the argument from sour grapes, and the poem successfully scores off himself, womankind, and the Petrarchan clichés.

Campion is amazingly consistent, especially in the *Book of Airs* which he published with a composer called Rossiter in 1601, the first half of which contains Campion's poems to his own setting. They form an impressive array. *My Sweetest Lesbia* (which it is worth comparing with Jonson's *Come, my Celia* in *Volpone*) is another poem urging the lady to enjoy physical pleasures while she still can; it is written in the shadow of a great Latin love poem by Catullus, *Vivamus, mea Lesbia*, and for those who can read

Latin, Campion's poem demonstrates the richness with which study of the classics could fertilise an English poet a millennium and a half later. But the poem is very distinguished in its own right, more serious than the one quoted and just as expert. His language never fails to perceive physical events with delicious accuracy, while it never over-indulges itself; it is limpid. He gives us the delights of sexuality with comedy and tenderness (particularly in *Turn Back, You Wanton Flier; Shall I come, Sweet Love*, and *It Fell on a Summer's Day*), and once or twice he modulates into a distincter gravity:

> When thou must home to shades of underground,
> And there arrived a new admiréd guest,
> The beauteous spirits do engirt thee round,
> White Iopë, blithe Helen, and the rest,
> To hear the stories of thy finished love
> From that smooth tongue whose music hell can move.
>
> Then wilt thou speak of banqueting delights,
> Of masques and revels which sweet youth did make,
> Of tourneys and great challenges of knights,
> And all these triumphs for thy beauty's sake:
> When thou hast told these honours done to thee,
> Then tell, O tell, how thou didst murder me.

The unforgettable first line promises a bleaker treatment than Campion provides. He deflects the course of that sombre pentameter into a crowded party of mythological film stars—it is an adroit way to work in the overworked compliment about the superiority of his mistress to Helen. But having created his party —'admired guest', 'beauteous spirits' 'engirding' the lady— Campion returns us to the charged severity with which he opens:

> From that smooth tongue whose music hell can move.

It is a bland, shocking line. Instantly he goes back to the language of chivalric fantasy—masques and tournaments and so on, so stylishly rehearsed in this reminiscent, urbane voice. Again, in the last line, a startling alteration of pressure registers itself in the slight displacement of stresses, the repetition,

> Then tell, O tell, how thou didst murder me.

It is as if Campion wanted to write a poem on more momentous themes than he had to hand. He possessed the technique, but did not look for the theme, and so he wrote a poem which disturbs us with a sense that something greater than is evident is going on behind the poem, and neither poet nor reader can make it out. The poem wants to be wider in scope and more considerable than it is. Something of the same thing seems to happen in the lovely song *Now Winter Nights Enlarge* but Campion controls the experience better, and ends with a light (but, one feels, truthful) disenchantment which recommends briefly enchanting pleasures like poetry, music, wine and love as antidotes to boredom. It represents a mild essay in hedonism, but it does not affect to generalise about life, only about ways of passing long December evenings, and consequently poem and theme are one, and the poem is perfect.

In one or two poems Campion tackles the bigger themes that bother him, notably in *To Music Bent Is My Retired Mind*, and in this:

> The cypress curtain of the night is spread,
> And over all a silent dew is cast.
> The weaker cares by sleep are conqueréd,
> But I alone, with hideous grief, aghast,
> In spite of Morpheus' charms, a watch do keep,
> Over mine eyes, to banish careless sleep.

> Yet oft my trembling eyes through faintness close,
> And then the map of hell before me stands,
> Which ghosts do see, and I am one of those
> Ordained to pine in sorrow's endless bands,
> Since from my wretched soul all hopes are reft,
> And now no cause of life to me is left.

> Grief, seize my soul, that will still endure,
> When my crazed body is consumed and gone;
> Bear it to thy black den, there keep it sure,
> Where thou ten thousand souls dost tire upon.
> But all do not afford such food to thee
> As this poor one, the worser part of me.

Campion's Petrarchanism rises here to magnificence. The familiar terms—insomnia (except he *wants* to sleep, but fears the terrible nightmare), 'Morpheus', 'trembling', 'faintness', 'sorrow', 'pine' and the rest—he calls to striking new service, and the result is very powerful. The command is absolute—consider the imperious insistence congruent upon dignity in 'Grief, seize my soul', the unearthly mixture of courage and terror and intention in

Bear it to thy black den, there keep it sure,

the nightmare evoked by 'tire'. We cannot doubt the authenticity of the experience; it is fully realised.

Yet although this poem demonstrates Campion's mastery of his style and although it coheres with the main line of his writing, it is exceptional and being so, one could not wish the substance of his work were other than it is. There are few poets who deal as he does with such austerity and grace in the sensuous, coy, playful, joyous and ironic. He is always serious, none the less, conscious of a maturer attitude than the poem itself may be describing, nearly faultless as to the ease with which he wears erudition and wit. The tact he brings to sexual feelings is a lesson to other ages which treat them, on the whole, mawkishly, stridently or with callousness, and the tact is a symptom of cultural health. Campion refines the eloquent style, and lends it free and intelligent play over the minor range of subjects he selected. His subjects limited him, and so no doubt did his temperament and talent. But inclining one way, he came very near a full reconciliation of the new poetry and the old, the native and the 'sugared'. At about the same time, Greville in a handful of poems, and Shakespeare, Donne and Ben Jonson in a great many, achieved that union.

6

The Style Perfected: Fulke Greville and Shakespeare

I have invoked Greville once or twice in earlier chapters and the name probably came as unfamiliar to some readers, for Greville's poetry is not widely known. In so far as this volume is an essay in literary criticism and not literary history (and if they are separate), then I want to make out a special case for Greville's unusual distinction as a poet, since the comparative neglect of his poetry leads to a misunderstanding of the making of English poetry, as it deprives us of reading a fine writer. The neglect is, moreover, a failure in literary history, for Greville was an active participant in the experimenting of the 'New Poetry' movement led by Sidney in the eighties, he was Sidney's closest friend, and while paying such generous tribute to Sidney in his biography he went some way towards extinguishing his own reputation by capturing the extraordinary and brilliant magnetism of the man his inferior as a poet. To enforce the contrast between the two of them, Greville wrote of himself:

> For my own part I found my creeping genius more fixed upon the images of life, than the images of wit, and therefore chose not to write to them on whose foot the black ox has not already trod, as the proverb is, but to those only that are weatherbeaten in the sea of this world, such as having lost the sight of their gardens and groves, study to sail on a right course among rocks and quicksands.
>
> LIFE OF THE RENOWNED SIR PHILIP SIDNEY

This cryptic utterance gives us a good deal to ponder. It properly suggests the prevailing gravity, tending to gloom, in Greville's poetry, and in its intent seriousness implies a certain impatience with the 'gardens and groves' bright and flowery with the 'images of wit', a puritan commitment to the poetry of sober certainty and wakefulness—to such a mind the only responsible kind if one must so study one's course among the awful hazards. Yet this joyless summary does Greville much less than justice. We might begin our study of his verse by recalling his (again tantalising) wish 'to be known to posterity under no other notion than of Shakespeare's and Ben Jonson's master'. 'No other notion', indeed! It is a colossal ambition, nonchalantly thrown out, yet Greville was never a man for needless exaggeration, canny in politics and grim in his verse. Given the muscular frame of his poetry, the ambition will perhaps come to look less outrageous. We do not know anything of Greville's contact with the two greatest poets of the age, but the evidence we have—the poems—deserves the most careful attention and, in view of our ignorance, drastic promotion. One way of beginning such study would be for the reader to compare a sonnet or two of Drayton's, with whom literary historians since their own time have tended to group Greville and Chapman, with one or two of Greville's: Drayton's *Since there's no help* perhaps, and Greville's *Caelica 38* or *40*. Greville's two poems are roughly Petrarchan in feeling, and they come in the first half of his sequence; Drayton's poem is not piffling. Yet Greville's show a much more resourceful technique at work, an ampler vocabulary, and an intelligence in one case richly scornful and in the other, gentle and elegiac. When, however, we reach the last forty or so poems in *Caelica* we confront a poet who has fully outgrown the early fancies and whose mind and sensibility, far outstripping those of a poet like Drayton, reach out and grapple with the central and metaphysical problems of experience. We find a master of technique and a master of a particular body of thought. The range of the poetry is not wide and is predominantly sombre, but it straddles some of the most important areas of our lives, and expresses attitudes of rare courage and clarity. If in the end we are bound to pass limiting judgments on Greville, it is because claims for him must take their stand on a handful of poems, and those poems themselves are so exclusively austere, repressive and absolute.

There are three details of the foregoing account which in order to thicken our sense of the Elizabethan context need fuller treatment. There is, first, the arrival in the poetry written after 1590 of a new and 'metaphysical' preoccupation. Second, there is the dependent pressure of the new, rebellious theologies, and in Greville's case particularly that of Jean Calvin from Geneva. Finally, Greville's poetry provokes a question already in part discussed in this volume in one or other of the poems, and prompting anxious queries about the poetry of today. What is meant by a 'public voice' in poetry? Does public authority in a poem matter at all? Is the 'public voice' now stilled? If so, does it matter? Questions of this sort enfold the whole life of a literature, and therefore a nation, and we cannot answer them only in discussion of Greville. But we should start to ponder them in the echo of his uniquely public authenticity, and worry once again about the paradoxical relations between private, handwritten Court poems and the unity of Elizabethan society.

The meaning of 'metaphysical' has had a good deal of airing (among other places, in Jim Hunter's volume *The Metaphysical Poets* in this series). Whatever meaning we finally ascribe to it, we must know that poetry which aspires to metaphysicality needs for its immediate inspiration a culture of zestful vitality, intellectually inexhaustible and busy with contradictions. And for adequate expression, such poetry must clearly need poetic techniques of refinement and subtlety, strong enough for grandeur, supple enough for wit. Metaphysical poetry (and prose) requires for its cultivation advanced conditions of civilisation. What is this thing that needs so elaborate, lengthy development? James Smith in an admirable essay offers a studiedly literal-minded definition:

> ... I prefer ... to venture upon my own definition of metaphysical verse. It is, that verse properly called metaphysical is that to which impulse is given by an overwhelming concern with metaphysical problems; with problems either deriving from, or closely resembling in the nature of their difficulty, the problem of the Many and the One. The definition sounds spare, but that I do not look upon as a defect. It is at any rate fairly clear.
>
> 'On Metaphysical Poetry', SCRUTINY II, p. 228

'Metaphysical', strictly analysed, means 'beyond the physical world', i.e. insoluble by the ordinary laws of physical behaviour. The classic metaphysical problem is the struggle to reconcile the chaotic details of experience with a desire for order and coherence, for making sense of the mess. Now only minds of a certain stamp are at all interested in the problem. Most of us get by without pushing the possible answers too far; sometimes, because we terribly want to believe in an ordered unity, we tussle awhile and find evidence that the unity is so; sometimes, we—or some one of us, a poet maybe, or a philosopher—try to believe we are part of a universal scheme of things, but it becomes too much of an effort, and we give up. We conclude there is only that which gives things as they are in the plentitude of fact, without imagination, without divine solicitude or human. It is in this desert place that one or two 20th-century metaphysicals end up. Like Wallace Stevens:

> The leaves cry. It is not a cry of divine attention,
> Nor the smoke-drift of puffed-out heroes, nor human cry.
> It is the cry of leaves that do not transcend themselves,
>
> In the absence of fantasia, without meaning more
> Than they are in the final finding of the ear, in the thing
> Itself, until, at last, the cry concerns no one at all.

THE COURSE OF A PARTICULAR

A metaphysical poet like Greville or Donne found a very different composure. They scrutinise the welter of day-to-day living, and seek to define the delicate balance of their minds between scepticism and moral certainty. The atmosphere of metaphysical poetry is thick with speculation, touched with scepticism, and yet sufficiently confident of its bearings to use moral language straightforwardly. There is no question, that is, that the words will break up in their hands. Such moments in a civilisation occur rarely and only when, as it were, society turns very slowly upon a fulcrum, or away from one pole towards another. You can see this happening in the thirty years from 1590 to 1620, with traces before and after. The old medieval absolutes were still walking the boards in the vivid figures of the Morality plays and allegories. They then start to mingle with new and daring intellectual ideas, and with scepticism. The result in the poems of a few men was an extraordinary combination of allegory and ideas, of fleshly and spiritual thinking and feeling. For we see in Greville and Donne, in the Shakespeare of a few sonnets, in *Henry IV, Troilus and Cressida, Hamlet, Lear, Timon* and elsewhere, and later in Jonson, Herbert and Marvell, ideas and thought take on an individual vividness such as they cannot show in later, more abstracted and conceptual thinking. The life realises in the language both precision and mobility. General abstractions can move with the suddenness of particular details. The poetry of metaphysical statement is also dramatic poetry, for in it the poet attains his sharp perception of the colliding components of the metaphysical problem. There is a straight line from the native tradition of moral-reflective poetry to the lucid, unambiguous metaphysics of Greville and beyond.

In Greville's case there was a further predisposition towards metaphysicality and moral reflection springing from his Calvinism. Where his friend Sidney was a Puritan, and, in spite of Penelope Devereux, owing duty to chastity, austerity, self-control and self-reliance, Greville took the same beliefs further into the camp of the extreme, intolerant and sometimes bigoted Calvinists. Calvin's theology started out from Geneva, and quarrelled even more violently with the traditional structure of Catholicism than Luther's had. Calvin taught a belief in predestination in which God chose the saved and dismissed the damned while they were still in this life, in which the line between moral good and bad was distinctly and absolutely drawn; consequently the penitent's act of conversion, though a desirable good, was the effect of God's inscrutable purpose and nothing at all to do with the individual. None the less, the diffused effects of Calvin's teaching were such as to endorse the new weight thrown on the individual's shoulders by Renaissance Humanism; even though his acts of penitence and salvation were involuntary according to the doctrine, the Calvinist's strenuous attention to his own soul, the importance of the moment in which he saw the light, his self-conscious rectitude and absence of any absolving ritual, concentrated his imagination upon a vision of simple, terrible, and overpowering finality. Greville's great intellectual triumph is to take this vision and unite it with the vision of a more complex and equable morality.

Finally, Greville carries off the note of public authority in his verse. His style depends on such antecedent writing as has made a public voice possible. Wyatt, Gascoigne, Ralegh, and others won the ground for him; so, pre-eminently, did the Elizabethan translations of the Bible. The point is made perhaps if we listen to the voice of T. S. Eliot in the *Four Quartets*. It is the voice of a man speaking to a small, intent, serious circle of listening friends; it is not 'public'. When we do find a modern poet, as we do in W. B. Yeats, who attempts to strike great public chords, we intermittently find hitches of tone, flatness, uncertainty, or rant. And we find in him an enormous regret that the days of public poetry may be gone for ever.

> O what if gardens where the peacock strays
> With delicate feet upon old terraces,
> Or else all Juno from an urn displays
> Before the indifferent garden deities;
> O what if levelled lawns and gravelled ways
> Where slippered Contemplation finds his ease
> And childhood a delight for every sense,
> But take our greatness with our violence?

MEDITATIONS IN TIME OF CIVIL WAR I

Well, what if? The section ends on the outflung question. Trying to form a large poem on large political issues, he does not know how to talk to whom. The same problem faced Wordsworth, so he talked to strange solitaries of Lakeland, or he spoke about himself. Keats, rejecting Wordsworth's 'egotistical sublime', abandoned *his* great vision *The Fall of Hyperion* because he could not sort out the conflicting claims of myth and self. Things were different for Greville, Shakespeare, Donne, Jonson, and after them (beyond the covers of this book) Herbert, Herrick and Milton. The donkeywork had been done: the style and the moment were ready together.

It would seem that Greville only realised this slowly. In

Sidney's wake, his sonnet-sequence *Caelica* (which means 'the heavens': contrast Sidney's 'Stella', the star) starts out with the familiar Petrarchan luggage, and although Greville makes more of this equipment than Drayton and writes some good sonnets, the love poetry lacks Sidney's tenderness and affection; Greville's mind, though allusive and artful, was elsewhere. His courtly flirtations and jests turn out cynical or scornful or plain moralising. So he is at his best when he withdraws a little to generalise:

> The nurse-life wheat, within his green husk growing,
> Flatters our hope and tickles our desire . . .

The odd, lively verbs mobilise the abstractions. The next sestet takes Ralegh's kind of bitterness and extends it to take in a brief, dramatic glimpse of the court life which provoked the poem:

> I from my paradise was straight forbidden—
>
> Where that cur, Rumour, runs in every place,
> Barking with Care, begotten out of Fear;
> And glassy Honour, tender of Disgrace,
> Stands Seraphin to see I come not there;
> While that fine soil, which all these joys did yield,
> By broken fence is proved a common field.

CAELICA 38

Greville's heritage, by way of medieval morality and Calvinist contempt for social hypocrisy, and by way of the native and Petrarchan poets, comes together and issues in an assured and excellent idiom. It is not the language but the action of the poem which is metaphysical. The language is plain, unPetrarchan. But a violent energy runs with this hybrid dog, Rumour, whose bark is care and whose breeding was allegorical. It is a fleshly rumour and a spiritual dog, and both at once. The same gifts quicken the odd paradoxes of the next two lines whose 'glassy' Honour stands guard, 'tender' of Disgrace to keep from violation a disgraced and violated heroine. After the clandestine drama of these lines, Greville releases the concealed regret, admiration and sardonic detachment of the poem beneath the coolness of the couplet.

But Greville is never fully at home with the tarnished glories of the Petrarchan manner. Not until he casts it off can he speak out in his own voice, when the power of that voice merges with the depth of his theme to create a fully religious and metaphysical poetry, and one which in spite of a narrow and frightful creed embodies a properly serious and impersonal publicity. *Caelica 69* is the first in his mature style. I hold it in spite of its unremitting bleakness one of the finest religious poems in English.

> When all this All doth pass from age to age,
> And revolution in a circle turn,
> Then heavenly Justice doth appear like rage,
> The caves do roar, the very seas do burn,
> > Glory grows dark, the sun becomes a night,
> > And makes this great world feel a greater might.
>
> When Love doth change his seat from heart to heart,
> And Worth about the wheel of fortune goes,
> Grace is diseased, desert seems overthwart,
> Vows are forlorn, and Truth doth credit lose,
> > Chance then gives law, Desire must be wise
> > And look more ways than one, or lose her eyes.
>
> My age of joy is past, of woe begun;
> Absence my presence is, strangeness my grace;
> With them that walk against me is my sun;
> The wheel is turned; I hold the lowest place.
> > What can be good to me, since my love is,
> > To do me harm, content to do amiss?

The last two lines disappoint us; they transpose the massive music of the poem and constitute something of a sellout to the old style. Greville has written an extremely remarkable poem, novel, audacious, yet deeply traditional, but he can't end it. Or he doesn't notice what it is he has made. What he gives us is a fully realised vision of spiritual desolation, the experience of a man from whom grace has withdrawn. It is not a private experience, nor an exclusively Christian one; it is universal and it is appalling. We might use psychological language and say that this poem realises and judges the acute coincidence of guilt and isolation known as paranoia. The poem is evidence that Greville has faced and defined the utter (and perhaps insane) desolation and has arrived at a moral attitude towards it, which is the poem itself. Consider how it is done. Behind each word one senses the push of great ranges of thought and feeling, one senses the history of the word. The irresistible splendour of the movement derives from the earlier Bible, yet it is distinctively Greville's own. The very general terms work, because the poem has such sweep:

When all this All doth pass from age to age,
And revolution in a circle turn—

the lines revolve around some gigantic axis before the momentum of the huge phrases, 'all this All', 'age to age'. Calvinism and honest guilt give us the sudden drama of the third line, and this mixture intensifies through the violent series of oxymorons, the colliding opposites:

The caves do roar, the very seas do burn,
  Glory grows dark, the sun becomes a night,
  And makes this great world feel a greater might.

The antitheses are completely lucid, the metaphors conventional, the language simple; yet their insistent accumulation through the poem makes for a feeling of pure terror. Greville's characteristic gift for animating his abstractions by restless paradox renders the contradictions of religious (and actual) experience, the inexplicable alternations of redemption and abandonment. There are many words made flesh in this poem, as in many of the mature Greville, but one of his finest lines is surely,

Absence my presence is, strangeness my grace.

Here in the most metaphysical way, the sober pentameter, the bare generalisation gather and clarify the resisting essences of the metaphysical problem. And the grave argument proceeds to the recognition, made without compromise:

The wheel is turned; I hold the lowest place.

Greville's poetry is the poetry of thought: the realisation in terms of thought and feeling of his intellectual experience. It is not merely a matter of 'knowing about' his intellectual heritage, it is a matter of command, and if *Caelica 69* is flawed by the uncertainty of the last couplet, the last thirty or so poems in the sequence are nearly beyond objection. He becomes aware, finally, of his proper subject-matter, and in a dignified sonnet takes his leave and discards the Petrarchan style:

> But, Cupid, now farewell; I will go play me
> With thoughts that please me less, and less betray me.
>
> CAELICA 84

I cannot here go through all the remaining poems of the sequence, though you may object that thirty or so is a smallish number on which to base such claims as I make. But the task of writing the perfect poem is very difficult, and few poets manage more than thirty. The case against Greville—which I shall put —depends on the quality, range, and humanity of the spirit evidenced in these poems. It is, relevantly enough, a moral case.

There are a number of his poems after the farewell in *84* I would like to consider. In spite of the sameness in treatment of his Calvinism, Greville irresistibly persuades the reader of the moving and *personal* permanence for him of this theology and its relations to an older morality. The reader might look up (poems by Greville aren't easy to find in the anthologies) the series of hymns written from the depths of humiliation pleading for salvation (*De Profundis Clamavi*, a traditional theme), numbers *88*, *98*, *99*, *109*, the very precise statement of moral nightmare in *100*, the vision of the apocalypse in *86*, and the very powerful rewriting of *69* (which I have quoted) in number *87*. In each of these short poems Greville shows himself in charge of the manner and the material. The manner (which is the man) is sombre, meditative, exact and confident; the material is unified and important. I shall end by considering *Caelica 98*.

> Wrapped up, O Lord, in man's degeneration,
> The glories of thy truth, thy joys eternal,
> Reflect upon my soul dark desolation,
> And ugly prospects o'er the sprites infernal.
>   Lord, I have sinned, and mine iniquity
>   Deserves this hell; yet, Lord, deliver me.
>
> Thy power and mercy never comprehended
> Rest lively imaged in my conscience wounded;

> Mercy to grace, and power to fear extended,
> Both infinite: and I in both confounded.
>> Lord, I have sinned, and mine iniquity
>> Deserves this hell; yet, Lord, deliver me.
>
> If from this depth of sin, this hellish grave,
> And fatal absence from my Saviour's glory,
> I could implore His mercy, who can save,
> And for my sins, not pains of sin, be sorry,—
>> Lord, from this horror of iniquity
>> And hellish grave, Thou wouldst deliver me.

One detail which rings oddly in our ears is the feminine rhyming ('degeneration'/'desolation'), but it is a constant device of Greville's and serves to soften the implacable march of his argument and rhythms. The rhythms of this poem are hymnal. Each stanza closes with a sort of refrain, but the refrain is woven tightly into the stuff of his argument so that the slight closing variation is enough to startle into feeling the momentous nature of the conclusion: 'Thou wouldst deliver me'. The pallor of this language is such that minor disturbances ruffle the liturgy with the anguish of individual experience. There is no joy in this poem. The glories and joys reflect only desolation, yet the grimness of Greville's courage gives the poem the strength, the bowels of tragedy. It is the tragedy of stoic Christianity, in which consolation is too immense to be useful. The expansive movement and breadth of concept in:

> Thy power and mercy never comprehended

preclude human understanding, but the devout, familiar language make the situation communal. The grand movement is checked on the colon, 'Both infinite', and the only certainty of the stanza seals its argument by a dreadful logic, realised in syntax, argument, rhythm and imagery: 'and I in both confounded'. It is Greville's gift to recharge this traditional liturgy with its proper grandeur and finesse. It is a matter of trusting the abstractions to do their work, in quickening them by minor changes and tiny personal insertions, and in suffusing their movement with his unique tone of voice: grave, deliberate and extremely moving:

In power and truth, almighty and eternal,
Which on the sin reflects strange desolation,
With glory scourging all the sprites infernal,
And uncreated hell with unprivation;
    Deprived of human graces, not divine,
    Even there appears this saving God of mine.

CAELICA 99

It is astonishing that anyone could make such powerful poetry out of spiritual privation. Here, again, the massive music of the great terms 'power' 'truth' 'almighty' takes precision and intensity from the strange paradoxes—'glory scourging', and the creator uncreating hell by depriving it of deprivation, a penetrating use of Aquinas's definition of evil as good starved of nourishment. Again, the stanza closes upon the dogged hope of redemption in spite of everything.

In the end, one withholds from Greville the highest praise. He is a weighty figure; he exemplifies the powerful play of an extraordinary intelligence. His vision is chilling and relentless, but it is unfailingly dignified, replete with courage. His technique is unimpeachable. But any complete attitude to life (which is what we ask of the great) demands that in setting aside the delights of life, they should be justly valued. Greville finds the delights wearisome, and joyful sympathy impossible. He lacks, I think, a sufficient notion of nobility.

WILLIAM SHAKESPEARE

Shakespeare's *Sonnets* have given rise to such an intolerable deal of biographical speculation that one cannot mention them without giving a very brief account of the most popular theories, and some description of the classifications possible within the total. Speculation begins with the notorious dedication page to the 1609 quarto edition (it would be superfluous here to estimate the validity of this text. Interested readers will find an admirably succinct account of general textual problems in editing Shakespeare in a companion volume in this series, *Shakespeare* by Grose and Oxley). The dedication reads:

112

TO. THE. ONLIE. BEGETTER. OF.
THESE. INSUING. SONNETS.
MR. W. H. ALL. HAPPINESSE.
AND. THAT. ETERNITY.
PROMISED.
BY.
OUR. EVER-LIVING. POET.
WISHETH.
THE. WELL-WISHING.
ADVENTURER. IN.
SETTING.
FORTH.

T. T.

Setting aside the weird punctuation, we may briefly summarise the claims laid to the initials. The publisher, who signed the dedication, was Thomas Thorpe, the title page is dated 1609, and it seems probable that Shakespeare himself had not authorised the edition: the order of the sonnets is wayward, the mistakes are such as an author would have corrected in a fair copy, and there is the puzzling fact that although Shakespeare was a celebrated author by 1609, there is little evidence of popular and rapid sales. It is suggested that because of the great names involved in the clandestine *affaires*, Thorpe had to suppress his edition. Whether or not this is a fair conjecture, it emphasises the mysterious privacy of the sonnets, both in their origins and interpretation. And the names involved were very famous. If we disregard the more eccentric theories advanced that Mr. W. H. was a publishing friend of Thorpe's or was one William Hews, a sea-cook, then the principal claimants are the Earl of Southampton, one of Shakespeare's earliest patrons, or the dazzling William Herbert, Earl of Pembroke, who died in 1630 after a career as a courtier, diplomat and patron, in which he was about equally famous for his amazing charm and intelligence, and for his abandoned sensuality. We cannot weigh all the evidence here, though scholarly preference is gathering more definitely behind the Earl of Pembroke; what is important is that Mr. W. H., if he is the 'onlie begetter' of the sonnets, is the friend to whom the variousness, passion and moral force of the sequence is given. This friend is clearly much younger than Shakespeare, is a great deal higher in the social scale, is a figure of intelligence, irresistible charm, and of intermittent callousness and voluptuousness. The Earl of Pembroke fits this account sufficiently well, but naming the friend is irrelevant to our main concerns. We need to grasp that the immediate reference of these poems is remarkably private —they are written at first for a single reader, and although their cumulative shape is grander than any such occasion warrants, the poems rarely carry the public authority of Greville's poetry. They seem to rest in the margins outside Shakespeare's most imperious and universal statements, yet they press on into uncharted parts of experience with an entirely novel audacity and fullness. Together, the *Sonnets* compose a sort of 'poetic investigations', a series of remarks which travel over a given field of thought and experience, criss-cross in every direction. The poems are, as it were, a number of sketches of landscapes which were made in the course of long and involved journeyings. Some of these are slight or flimsy, some just elegant little affairs thrown out for the sociable moment, some mystify us by their obscurity or by particularly personal advice and prompt us not so much to interest in poetry as in gossip. But a biggish number of the sonnets, scattered at unpredictable intervals but becoming more frequent beyond about 50, speak out with a confidence, purity and exactitude which clear the private situation and evince the consummate union of theme and style which issues in the command of genius. A critic writing in 1598 of 'mellifluous and honey-tongued Shakespeare' admired 'his sugared sonnets among his private friends', and by 'sugared' he meant the eloquent style, the lofty manner of high Renaissance England. But the greatest sonnets are not sugared; they attain a perfect adjustment of sweetness and softness to lucidity and sudden intellectual force. There are, besides, a large number which haunt us more strangely with a sense of pervasive but indescribable threat. It is my business in this chapter to name a few of the sonnets which approach or attain success.

There is no room therefore to make an exhaustive classification of the sonnets. In order to urge how perplexing this would be, it is worth briefly listing the possible themes which one may trace through the sequence. In fact, it is misleading to call it a sequence at all, if this implies (as it does for Sidney's *Astrophel and Stella* and Spenser's *Amoretti*, though not for Greville) a planned development. As I have said, what we find, though richly interrelated, is a network of resemblances and extensions. These arise from a particular intention. The first seventeen sonnets attempt to persuade the friend to marry and have children. It may be that the nobleman's family commissioned Shakespeare to write this in order to encourage the Earl of Pembroke (or whomever) to remember his dynastic duties, but however it was, the poet quickly transcended the formal intentions and moved into the sonnets *18–126* which explore the wretchedness and exaltation of his relationship with his magnetic friend. Within this group lie smaller groups on different topics, such as *87–93* all of which take farewell of the friend, and *78–86* all of which (apart from *81*) deal in some way with the claims of a rival poet to the friend's affection. Hidden in the main group are sonnets *40–2* which prefigure the concluding section of the sonnets, numbers *127–52*, and deal with Shakespeare's passion for his mistress, the 'Dark Lady' who may have been the court Maid of Honour whom Pembroke seduced but who was certainly fickle and coquettish enough to allow the friend to supplant Shakespeare in her bed.

These are some of the divisions possible in the total. But there are many more classifications which cut across these divisions into topic or occasion. We could group together those sonnets which celebrate the triumph of Love over Time, and those which flinch before the converse; we could group together poems of moral introspection and condemnation, those of loss, regret and desolation, and those of joy and fulfilment. A variety of groupings are possible, yet the range of experience explored in the sonnets is not strikingly wide. If the onward ranging of the spirit in these 152 poems (the last two are of doubtful ascription) is more quick and mobile than the intent, undeviating march of the later Greville, yet there is not in Shakespeare's sonnets the same compass and inclusiveness, the profundity and polish that we find in the complete poems of Ben Jonson. And this is partly because Shakespeare seemed to confine his intentions in these poems, partly that he wrote them fairly early in his career. There is a mixture of evidence for dating them—of internal critical evidence ('This sounds like *Henry IV*; that is better written than *Richard II*; surely these poems are less mature than *King Lear*'), and of references to external events, such as an anniversary of the Spanish Armada and recent political upheavals such as the Gunpowder Plot. In spite of this latter, however, a majority of literary historians seems inclined to settle the writing of the sonnets somewhere in between 1595 and 1600, that is to say during the years in which he composed (among others) *A Midsummer Night's Dream, I Henry IV, Twelfth Night* and *Julius Caesar*.

Any valuation of the poems which (as it might) set them below Jonson, Herbert and Donne should beware of selling the sonnets short. For Shakespeare is sorting the travails of a new moral sensibility, searching for a delicate equipoise between the claims of the secure moral tradition in which he grew up and the impassioned demands of his own more unstable, vulnerable England. There is in Shakespeare as in no one else in literature a quite terrific openness and responsiveness to experience. His sense of identity is so capacious that he can risk more than a 'closed' poet, a poet whose moral judgments are more definite because they don't let so much in. Many readers besides myself have found something of the same thing in Keats, but brutally cut off, of course, at twenty-six. It is there in Herbert and Marvell. This openness is the main characteristic of the poems to the friend. I am not trying to whitewash Shakespeare in saying that these are not homosexual poems, but trying to define a quality which cannot be constricted by the narrower implications of 'homosexual'. Rather, Shakespeare takes to astounding extremes something we all feel when we first meet friends who overpower us with a sense of magnetism, intelligence, colour. They briefly fill us with a sense of themselves and their gifts, and we lose sight of ourselves in an odd, choky kind of excitement. We look forward tremendously to seeing them. The Shakespearean version of what is, I take it, a not uncommon experience is given in these lines by a modern poet about Michelangelo. Since Michelangelo is one of the tiny number of European artists we might group beside Shakespeare it is important that these lines have an historical as well as a poetic truth. I think one could adduce more parallels from Mozart's letters.

> For you must know I am of all men ever born
> Most inclined to love persons, and whenever I see someone
> Who has gifts of mind and body, and can say or show me something
> Better than the rest,
> Straightway I am compelled
> To fall in love with him, and then I give myself
> Up to him so completely, I belong no longer to myself,
> He wresting from me
> So great part of my being, I am utterly
> Bewildered and distraught, and for many days know nothing
> Of what I am doing or where I am.
>
> F. T. Prince, 'The Old Age of Michelangelo', DOORS OF STONE, p. 83

This comes near the quality of Shakespeare's feeling for the friend. Now he relates to this feeling an ineffable and pervasive consciousness of the pressure of time, and he feels the combination of the two values as almost fleshly. It leads to poetry of quite extraordinary density, in which the suggestive power of something undefined but omnipresent packs the ostensible matter of the poem with significance. And sometimes the significance is severe and terrific, and sometimes baffling, sometimes awesome, and once or twice it is joyous. Shakespeare gives us, in other words, poetry of intense sensuous texture in which lovely detail is charged with a meaning beyond itself, a meaning, moreover, which the rational mind cannot identify but which we feel as pregnant, portentous and withheld.

Let me try to exemplify the stages by which Shakespeare seems to regress from meaning as he intensifies power of feeling. 23 is more graceful and skilled than many of Sidney's sonnets; Shakespeare organises it with a correct eloquence, well-placed indulgence and gentle self-deprecation. It is perfectly minor in key, phrasing, and theme.

As an unperfect actor on the stage,
Who with his fear is put besides his part,
Or some fierce thing replete with too much rage,
Whose strength's abundance weakens his own heart;
So I, for fear of trust, forget to say
The perfect ceremony of love's rite,
And in mine own love's strength seem to decay,
O'ercharged with burden of mine own love's might.
O, let my books be then the eloquence
And dumb presagers of my speaking breast,
Who plead for love, and look for recompense,
More than that tongue that more hath more expressed.
  O, learn to read what silent love hath writ:
  To hear with eyes belongs to love's fine wit.

SONNET 23

We have rightly admired these gifts elsewhere. *Sonnet 19*, however, is two halves of two much larger poems, magnificent in manner, bold and generous in phrasing and gesture; but the two halves do not make one poem. We have the first:

Devouring Time, blunt thou the lion's paws,
And make the earth devour her own sweet brood;
Pluck the keen teeth from the fierce tiger's jaws,
And burn the long-lived phoenix in her blood;
Make glad and sorry seasons as thou fleet'st,
And do whate'er thou wilt, swift-footed Time,
To the wide world and all her fading sweets,
But I forbid thee one most heinous crime . . .

Many people have noted how Shakespeare revives the Ovidian tag *Tempus edax rerum* ('Time the devourer of things') by the introduction of the lion (the biter bit). Shakespeare stresses the abrupt verbs 'blunt' after the comma, 'Pluck' at the start of the line, and the long glowing vowels and running consonants in the fourth line. Maybe the sixth line is the finest, almost bare as it is of figure, yet desperately plaintive in its openhanded gesture:

And do whate'er thou wilt, swift-footed Time.

The imperative is helpless before the quick beat of the cliché, alive again and busy, 'swift-footed Time'.

The eighth line falters into coyness—'But I forbid thee one most heinous crime'—and the poem is marred. After that he replaces the generalised magnificence with a new and tender poem not about the rapidity of Time but about a single person. The choice and placing of 'antique' gives poignancy to the sweet simplicity of the lines. The nearly imperceptible coarsening of tone in the couplet damages in turn the preceding lines. Shakespeare comes near the perfection of the style, but as he learns to master the matter as well as sustain his tone he seems to find that the themes burst apart the sonnet. He involuntarily crosses the limits of what can be said, as he remains so amazingly responsive to all he has heard. During the journey he discovers the perfect way of saying what was to be said before finding that there was yet more. In the end he had to discard the sonnet, but before then he practised and refined a method in which his genius barely surmounts the dangers he admitted. Here is a flawless sonnet:

> That time of year thou mayst in me behold
> When yellow leaves, or none, or few do hang
> Upon those boughs which shake against the cold,
> Bare ruined choirs where late the sweet birds sang.
> In me thou see'st the twilight of such day
> As after sunset fadeth in the west,
> Which by and by black night doth take away,
> Death's second self that seals up all in rest.
> In me thou see'st the glowing of such fire,
> That on the ashes of his youth doth lie,
> As the death-bed whereon it must expire,
> Consumed with that which it was nourished by.
>   This thou perceiv'st, which makes thy love more strong,
>   To love that well which thou must leave ere long.

SONNET 73

There is a hint in the incomparable fourth line—

Bare ruined choirs where late the sweet birds sang—

of the seductive power of sensuous detail (the detail itself provided by the monasteries sacked at the dissolution, half a century before). The melancholy music, the haunting image of cathedral chancels picked up in the rich collusion of 'choir' and 'sang', the vision of lovely ruins still echoing to the music of summer: these images drift into the imagination to the languid step of the rhythm, and stay there. Their beauty is such that the evocation is almost stronger than what it means. But not quite. It realises with so much calmness the dissolution of identities contemplated in the poem, but the line, the poem, and the poet retain their single identity.

The structure of the poem is repetitive; each quatrain repeats and slightly modifies the statement of the first. But each quatrain is extremely beautiful in its own (independent) right. Moribund metaphors (death as night and as a dying fire) come to life again, pointed by the lovely cadences ('As after sunset fadeth in the west') and the slight, correct paradox—

Consumed with that which it was nourished by.

The metaphors are not so striking that they catch attention in their own right, but enough to render concretely the experience of the poem. The final couplet does not weaken the poem by confining its relevance merely to friend or mistress. It remains at the level of momentous and dignified generalisation. The style of the poem is as pure as it may be; the subject is important. The rhythmic and metaphorical disturbances are adjusted to the meaning, and the feeling is powerful and discreet. The poem speaks of a universal experience with piercing individuality; it is alive to any man of any age, free of all dated apparatus, absolute and itself.

It is a wonderful poem. It does all that a sonnet can do, but Shakespeare's spirit was restless and he would have his sonnets do more. And here I must begin by referring the reader to William Empson's endlessly subtle reading of a handful of sonnets in *Seven Types of Ambiguity* (pp. 50–7). He throws up a large number of representative ambiguities in which Shakespeare uses a sort of 'fluid and interpenetrating unity' in which 'phrases go either with the sentence before or after and there is no break in the movement of the thought'. There is a simple example in *42*, one of the three sonnets about the mistress in the first 126.

Thou dost love her, because thou know'st I love her,
And for my sake even so doth she abuse me,
Suffering my friend for my sake to approve her,

> If I lose thee, my loss is my love's gains,
> And losing her, my friend hath found that loss . . .

The third line of the quotation may refer backwards or forwards, to 'she' or 'I', and although this is not a special example, the ambiguity creates a slight irony. *Sonnet 58* is more violently ambiguous—but I should quote Empson's analysis. It is extremely concise, and paraphrase would be foolish:

> O let me suffer (being at your beck)
> The imprisoned absence of your liberty,
> And patience tame, to sufferance bide each check,
> Without accusing you of injury.
> Be where you list, your charter is so strong
> That you yourself may privilege your time,
> To what you will, to you it doth belong,
> Yourself to pardon of self-doing crime.

> *And patience tame* expresses petulance by its contraction of meaning ('suffer tame patience'); 'be patience-tame', as in iron-hard; and 'tame patience', as in *bide each check*; followed by a rush of equivocal words, clinched with *belong*, which has for subject both *your time* and *to pardon* and implies, still with sweetness and pathos (it is an extraordinary balance of feeling), 'that is all I could have expected of you'.

SEVEN TYPES, p. 54

I would like to extend this consideration of ambiguity into one or two sonnets where I find Shakespeare braving experiences which remain cloudy and menacing, muttering behind the extraordinary beauty of the visible scenery. These sonnets are strong, they move invincibly in the mind, they stir tempestuously in the imagination; but I do not know properly what they are about, and if the fault is theirs, they are to that extent deficient. Something of this strangeness flickers within the shimmering images, the bemused tone of the first quatrain in *53*:

> What is your substance, whereof are you made,
> That millions of strange shadows on you tend?
> Since every one hath, every one, one shade,
> And you, but one, can every shadow lend.

The strangeness is there in the sumptuousness, the magnificence or the mystery which threaten to overwhelm by a single line or two the argument of a whole sonnet:

> And patience tame, to sufferance bide each check . . .
>
> 58
>
> Lilies that fester smell far worse than weeds.
>
> 94
>
> Not mine own fears, nor the prophetic soul
> Of the wide world dreaming on things to come . . .
>
> 107
>
> Ah, yet doth beauty like a dial hand
> Steal from his figure, and no pace perceived . . .
>
> 104

(where it isn't clear exactly how the stealing or the stealing away is done; the minute hand after all stays on the clock)

> The injuries that to myself I do
> Doing thee vantage, double-vantage me . . .
>
> 88
>
>   all things rare
> That heaven's air in this huge rondure hems . . .
>
> 21
>
> How sweet and lovely dost thou make the shame
> Which, like a canker in the fragrant rose,
> Doth spot the beauty of thy budding name . . .
>
> 95
>
> The expense of spirit in a waste of shame
> Is lust in action.
>
> 129
>
> That I have frequent been with unknown minds . . .
>
> 117

In each of these quotations there seems to me a sort of dizzy moment in the statement, and in the rhythm which is part of the statement, when Shakespeare spins away from the central core of the thought out into a nameless, amorphous area of experience where one cannot follow. The poem teeters for a moment and then settles again about its proper axis. It is not just a matter of struggling to express complex thoughts, it is a matter of a momentary, exhilarating and uncontrollable loss of identity.

The thing happens in *Sonnet 77*. The first six lines dedicate in grave and straightforward language the gift of an empty commonplace book. Gradually the theme shifts to encompass the record of time passing reflected by the mirror and the book:

> Thou by thy dial's shady stealth may know
> Time's thievish progress to eternity.

The theme of the sonnet stretches a little, but not unduly. In the next four lines, however, we find a statement about the baffling contradictions in the act of writing which, taken literally, must frighten us a great deal:

> Look! what thy memory cannot contain
> Commit to these waste blanks, and thou shalt find
> Those children nursed, delivered from thy brain,
> To take a new acquaintance of thy mind.

The invitation is offered to perceive what it is the memory cannot contain, because of its size or its inhumanity, and to set it down on the 'waste blanks', the smooth and impassive surface of the paper which is also the vacant desert of experience. Once recorded, relieved of the weight which the memory could not contain, one may take new stock of what is written, of one's own identity and the impersonal voids beyond. One cannot tell whether Shakespeare welcomes the disencumbrance as a therapy ('delivered from thy brain'), or whether the 'acquaintance' thus gained serves as a definition of self in the vast inane. In spite of this difficulty the language seems to combine plainness with the greatest possible precision; the rhythms are controlled but urgent, the air one of persuasive lucidity as of sound moral generalisation. This calmness only enhances the violent discomposure of the effect. The discomposure of poet and reader recurs through the sonnets. It is as though Shakespeare is troubled by something equivocal in experience, that this something haunts and eludes him, and he can only treat it by trying to record its sensuous, actual effect on him. Time and again, one's impression of a sonnet is made up about equally of confusion and power, and both in large measure. The suggestiveness of the sequence is illimitable, but the definition, the finished hardness of statement which the Renaissance poet looked for, is not always there. The reader may care to struggle with one or two of the sonnets which contain this magical and pervasive obliquity; I think he will find it in numbers *16, 83, 88, 121,* as well as those already mentioned. But I would like to conclude this chapter by briefly considering another of the fully achieved sonnets; those which define by example the triumph Shakespeare sought. It is justice that counts; a justice of logic, statement, image and movement, in which the experience of writing (and reading) the poem enables the most perfect understanding of the subject. Such an understanding does not blink the complexities of the subject, but it tries to get clear the obscure and ambiguous parts. Ambiguous poems are attractive and teasing, but they may also be unfinished; the poet has not completed the poem. *Sonnet 64* is as complete as it may be:

> When I have seen by Time's fell hand defaced
> The rich-proud cost of outworn buried age;
> When sometime lofty towers I see down-razed,
> And brass eternal slave to mortal rage;
> When I have seen the hungry ocean gain
> Advantage on the kingdom of the shore,
> And the firm soil win of the watery main,
> Increasing store with loss and loss with store;
> When I have seen such interchange of state,
> Or state itself confounded to decay;
> Ruin hath taught me thus to ruminate,
> That Time will come and take my love away.
> > This thought is as a death, which cannot choose
> > But weep to have that which it fears to lose.

Once more, the subject that possesses Shakespeare is Time. The first ten lines (as in *73*) state, restate and restate again the action of Time. The third quatrain breaks the argument in the second half to move towards the first conclusion—

> That Time will come and take my love away.

The couplet describes the poet's response to this perception. The movement of the pentameters is slow and grand (there is the faintest awkwardness in the third line); the images are adjusted to the argument, but they are resonant—'Time's fell hand' 'And brass eternal slave to mortal rage'—they are vivid but not obtrusive; complexities, as in the eighth line, are cleared but not simplified. The poem moves with increasing certainty to lines eleven and twelve:

> Ruin hath taught me thus to ruminate,
> That Time will come and take my love away.

And at this, I feel there is no more to be said. One need only quote the lines, and say (hands flung up, eyes wide) 'look!' Keats felt the same thing in a letter to a close friend:

> One of the three Books I have with me is Shakespeare's Poems: I neer found so many beauties in the Sonnets—they seem to be full of fine things said unintentionally—in the intensity of working out conceits. Is this to be borne? Hark ye! [and he quotes from *Sonnet 12*]
>
> To Reynolds, 22 November 1817

That is absolutely the response. 'Is this to be borne?' For there is in this sonnet an almost intolerable poignancy; the sweetness of the last two lines offers more than summary and much more than (as in too many sonnets) a trite return to the nominal situation. The couplet at once summarises and extends the experience, and does so with simplicity.

> This thought is as a death, which cannot choose
> But weep to have that which it fears to lose.

Such accuracy of thought and feeling is only possible in rhythms of such fluent beauty. Loveliness and morality become truth.

Keats's comments on the sonnets suggest an attractive way of writing about them. As he says of them elsewhere, 'How can I help bringing to your mind the line', and indeed one richly satisfying way of description would be just to quote and quote the innumerable, famous lines which roll out even where a whole sonnet may not succeed. The opulence and amplitude of manner and language overwhelm us; one goes down before the music.

Of course, there are plenty of clichés—the tiresome puns, as in *116* ('. . . when first your eye I eyed'), the sentimental lark in *29*, the 'rosy lips' of *116*, the punning on 'Will' in *135*—many of the sonnets are hasty, and many given up to slight ceremonies or Petrarchan sentimentality. But reading them straight through, as we should, we may separate first those poems which are as nearly perfect as poems can be. They are rich and civilised in every detail; they offer permanent touchstones of value throughout our experience, they become essential parts of our lives. These poems are in the central tradition of English literature; they help to create its central style; they compose with their fellows the wisdom of the race. And in Shakespeare's sequence we may distinguish secondly poems which are of such power we cannot miss them, but whose intentions and procedure, reaching out towards unbroken regions, issue in equivocation, elusiveness, danger and panic. They threaten to overturn this poet and any poet, and poets are, in Shelley's phrase, 'the unacknowledged legislators of the world'. Shakespeare mastered these dangers in the end, but the conflict took him out of short poems and back to the drama, where he remained. His genius was proof against the dangers of dramatic writing and so his plays are the greatest pieces of literature we have; but if, as I have urged, the short poem is potentially the greatest literary form and makes for the most unmistakable successes, it is worth looking for a poet whose short poems were the centre of his life, and who, sharing all that the Elizabethan moment had to give, created a finished body of work in his short poems. An array of writers claim this kind of attention between 1590 and 1650 or so: the first geniuses, Donne, Marvell, George Herbert, and hardly lesser, Carew and Greville, Henry Vaughan and Lord Herbert of Cherbury. I wish now to give pride of place in this book to Ben Jonson. It is a bold proposal, but I would set him above all the poets just listed and all those in their short poems whom I have discussed in earlier chapters. He is not given as much attention as he deserves, yet his poems seem to me the most central, and fully human of his time. If I justify these claims, then his is a formative voice in the English identity. Let us listen to him, and see.

26

7

Jonson the Master: Stones Well Squared

Given the eminence I ascribe to Jonson, it seems right that this chapter should open with a brief biography. But the decision is not only a critical one; Jonson occupies a position of unusual historical importance, and since we lack so much of the biographical evidence for Shakespeare whose career would be important in similar ways, Jonson's life is one of the few of which we can describe enough to know what life was like for a full-time professional in the world of letters. For Jonson, like Shakespeare, lacked Sidney's advantages of birth and ignored the particular aspirations of Ralegh or Donne. After his early years he was a full-time writer, and he was fiercely proud of it and censorious of amateurs; he was neither a churchman nor a politician (which is not to say he neglects political and theological action). He is an early representative of spectacular success in a new social group—the independent writers, though his independence, which was vigorously temperamental as well as social, was qualified by patronage, censorship, and the powers of the aristocracy.

The success he won depended in his youth on access to social opportunity. One or two literary historians have made much of Jonson's origins as a bricklayer, and this may be misleading. His father, who died a month before Jonson's birth in 1572, was a clergyman; his stepfather was a master-bricklayer, and as a craft-master a man of some social standing. None the less it would seem that his concerns were strictly non-intellectual, for after Jonson had been sent (sponsored apparently by a family friend) to the great London grammar school at Westminster, his stepfather removed him shortly before he would have entered the sixth form to proceed to Oxford or Cambridge. The record of his life between leaving school and turning up in the London theatre in 1597 is rather blurred. He was briefly a soldier in the Flemish wars which lingered on through the last two decades of the century and which killed Sidney. No doubt he enlisted when he was hard up, but from his acquaintance Drummond's report and his own *Epigrams 107* and *108* he was a forthright, competent soldier. During the missing years he also married a wife whom he later left, crisply describing her to Drummond as 'a shrew, yet honest', and fathered the two children whose deaths, at six months and seven years, prompted the two finest short epitaphs in the language (p. 146).

In 1598, after joining the famous manager Henslowe's company in London, Jonson arrived dramatically in the news: his play *Every Man in His Humour* won a striking success, and he was prosecuted for murder. The play was the first of a line of vivid, original and penetrating comedies, each (apart from the last two or three) remarkable for boisterous knockabout and also for moral stringency solidly there in the clear, penetrating light which the judgment of the plays sheds upon human affairs. We cannot consider the plays here, but it is important to say that, in all their exuberance and inventiveness of characterisation one never loses sight of their maker and his steady scrutiny of moral behaviour. The tone of the plays and of the poems is extraordinarily consistent, and it is one which, while taking high delight in the peculiarities of the subject, is always poised to move easily into judgment. It is magisterial but never frosty. Jonson's moral judgments, which may be highly-coloured and angry, or may be coolly judicious, arise from his boundless vitality, his keen sense of actual living. It is not surprising that Dickens admired Jonson's plays so much, and the plays and the poems are an entity; the work is the man.

The man was often an uncomfortable person to have around. Innumerable figures in his plays lampoon lesser rivals of the time, and he attacks them not only for stupidity and incompetence, but also for brute ignorance of the classical texts Jonson learned at Westminster and in which he so fully saturated his intelligence throughout his working life. The great teacher, classicist and historian William Camden taught Jonson at Westminster and, as that moving brief tribute *To Camden* (*Epigram 14*) makes clear, Camden remained teacher and friend to Jonson for many years. Jonson remade the tradition of the ancient classics in his own terms and with tremendous intensity; he made the breadth and variety of that tradition his own possession, and it grew with him according to the lineaments of his personality. So in his work a whole tradition—the great tradition of Christian humanism— utters through a distinctive and inimitable voice.

Just how broad and varied is the work we can only see if we read through the canon—plays, masques and poems, summarised and commented on during his last bedridden years between about 1630 and 1637 in his prose commonplace book, *Timber, or Discoveries*. The greatest comedies, *Volpone* (1606), *The Alchemist* (1612), *The Silent Woman* (1609) and *Bartholomew Fair* (1614), receive their acknowledgment as a part of literature; the extremely powerful political drama *Sejanus* (1605) is underrated and deserves more reading: the stately Court masques which Jonson provided for his admiring patron King James, all of which contain bold, rich and sometimes lovely poems, are scarcely read at all. Yet they are a large part of Jonson's work, and no adequate appraisal of his craftsmanship, as well as that part of him which enjoyed sumptuousness and splendour, is possible without at least a reading of the *Masque of Beauty* (1608) and *The Golden Age Restored* (1615–16). In spite of the extent of his work and wide-spread ignorance of so much of it, I would argue that one comes most definitely to the heart of his greatness in a close scrutiny of the poems, and that this opinion, as the conversations with Drummond and *Timber* imply, would have been Jonson's as well. The rest of the work is part of his plenitude and vitality, but if the case for the short poem is secure and if it does provide best for the poet's gifts, then Jonson's poems supply the essential evidence for the critic, the historian, and the human being.

Jonson's manifold humanity becomes explicit in the poems. In part this explicitness is merely anecdotal and, though of absorbing autobiographical interest, not really a part of our study. Thus, after his satire on the trendsetters and the swinging young charlatans-about-London *The Poetaster* was performed in 1601, the uproar which followed obliged him to publish a palliating prologue. But the prologue was as bluntly outspoken and independent as the play, and Jonson (as he well knew) appeased nobody. The same bluntness transpires after the flop of *The New Inn* in 1629 when he published the *Ode to Himself*, fulminating bitterly upon the grossness of his critics and the persecution of his gifts. Time and again Jonson had to call upon his patrons for rescue from the embarrassment incurred by his own proper failure to mitigate censure of the stupid, arrogant or wicked. He spoke out without compromise, and made the payment demanded. There was probably an element of deliberate self-sacrifice in all this, as there must be in anyone who sets up as a candid, incorruptible moral critic, as there must be perhaps in any kind of lonely hero. And there is no doubt that Jonson was such a hero. The age which lacks its Ben Jonson, its Dr. Johnson, its Charles Dickens, its F. R. Leavis, has no conscience, and its moral sense atrophies.

But what matters to us is not the actual historical occasions, though these are fascinating, but the poems in which the history is grasped in terms of moral realities. These poems delineate the moral pattern latent within the accidents of his life, and construct from them a generalised coherence. In saying that, I do not mean that he falsified his life in the interests of an ideal order of experience, but that the details and the proper names in the poems don't finally matter. What matters is that the poems are rooted in a real life; the experience and the personality from which they grow are solid and deep, and in recognising this, we recognise the rare integrity which can so put the truth of the poems beyond question. Jonson's poems provide a case in which we know from the art what the man was like, and the qualities realised in the art are those of a remarkably strong man, generous and abundant in his life, not gifted in speculative dialectic nor a glittering wit, but direct, independent, loyal and plainspoken. Thus it is affirmative evidence which the context of the poems gives us. Jonson became the leader of a literary club, having long been the magnetic centre of literary London as it met in the intellectual public houses. The club called itself 'The Tribe of Ben' and the quality of the poems it provoked makes it clear how gaping a distance lies between it and (say) the intellectual gossip-mongers of colour-supplement London. 'The Tribe of Ben' counted fine poets like Carew, Godolphin and Herrick among its number, and among the rest some of the most penetrating intelligences of the time—Lord Falkland, William Cavendish, Sir Kenelm Digby. It met for food, drink, and talk at the feet of the master, and the terms of its relationships were such as to provide rich and large material for poetry. The human contact signalled in *An Epistle, Inviting a Friend to Supper* deserves cherishing. There seems no reason why such experience should not persist.

Jonson was the last of the great Elizabethans. He *was* the tradition to which the new poets turned, and his statements carried an oracular weight. The prose commonplaces in *Timber* and the notes Drummond made during Jonson's visit to his Scottish home near Edinburgh in 1618 (Jonson walked there and back, from London, and stopped, fairly enough, each way in Darlington to buy new boots) serve as commentary both to the historical context in which the poems were written, and to their literary intention. There is not space to quote extensively from *Timber* or the *Conversations*, though it is worth turning back to the longish quotation on p. 17. A handful of remarks must serve to represent their characteristic inflexion and the tips they offer as to how to read both Jonson's and any other poetry, and to indicate how Jonson himself went to work, and what were his points of reference. Drummond thinly notes that in the first place Jonson was 'jealous of every word and action of those about him (especially after drink which is one of the elements in which he liveth)' (*Conversations 19*). The closest work and arguing went with canary wine as much as did the parties in the Devil Inn and the theatres. One recollection is challenging:

(15) his opinion of verses
　　　that he wrote all his first in prose, for so his
　　　master Camden had learned him.
　　　That verses stood by sense without either colours or accent,
　　　which yet other times he denied.

It sorts well with what we can see in his poems that they should start out from prose beginnings—as Ezra Pound wrote, 'poetry should be at least as well written as prose'. The poems intend a statement, and the original force of that statement inheres first in its 'sense', and if in Jonson's case the distinctive 'accent' of his 'sense' is inseparable from the sense itself, yet his deliberate strength is first a matter of moral force so that 'colours', figures of speech and elegance of numbers are subordinate. It is consistent that Jonson felt 'couplets to be the bravest sort of verses especially when they are broken and that cross rhymes and stanzas . . . were all forced' (1), and from this judgment it follows that 'Donne for not keeping of accent deserved hanging' (3) and that although 'he esteemeth John Donne the first poet in the world in some things' (7) 'Donne himself for not being understood would perish' (12). Jonson always intends clarity and the cutting away of ambiguity and obscurity from around the lines of the verse. The couplet makes for such hardness and precision, hence his preference (though Jonson, like most of his contemporaries, was a virtuoso in stanza forms).

There is only agreeable gossip value in pursuing Jonson's impenitent self-esteem—'That next himself only Fletcher and Chapman could make a masque' (3) and (accurately) 'he was better versed and knew more Greek and Latin than all the poets in England'. The last anecdotes ring with utter authenticity of his pigheaded bluntness and his robust independence, for 'he never esteemed of a man for the name of a Lord' (14):

> Jones [Inigo, with whom Jonson collaborated in Court masques] having accused him for naming him behind his back a fool, he denied it; 'But', says he, 'I said he was one arrant knave and I avouch it'.
> 17

> Being at the end of my Lord Salisbury's table with Inigo Jones and demanded by my lord why he was not glad, 'My Lord', said he, 'you promised I should dine with you, but I do not . . .'
> 13

These last extracts do no more than endorse the tones of the more relevant literary observations we have seen. In turning to *Timber*, we find the same tones meditating far more serious issues. It is notable that in dozens of places *Timber* is a rewriting, idea for idea, of some of the great classical critics and theorists of literature, particularly as they were rephrased for the Renaissance by the critic Vivès whose primers ran into dozens of editions and were certainly among the textbooks at Westminster School. But *Timber* is more than an annotation of Vivès's theories: it is the redefinition of Vivès in Jonson's cadences and with the weight of his experience behind the sentences. We do not need Drummond's reminder to know how close lay the rhythms of Jonson's verse and prose.

The quality of *Timber* cannot, I suppose, be fully judged without a reading of Vivès's *De Disciplinis* (1531), a grand formulation of all that was best in classical humanism. But the matter opens again the question of Jonson's relation to his history, and the way the history and the man moved together. I quote Wallace Stevens's noble poem *The House Was Quiet and the World Was Calm* in the last chapter during an attempt to define our understanding of a particular poetic tradition, and the decisive choices we make in charting our tradition. The analysis I propose (p. 159) may apply to Jonson, in *Timber* and in many poems. The scrapbook of quotations is tightened and compacted beneath the conviction of the writer. Each reminiscence from Vivès moves into the bone of Jonson's being; the teacher becomes the pupil, and the pupil surpasses the teacher in passion and intelligence. Thus continuity holds through. It is as though we read a gifted modern poet whose mind has sharply altered according to his response to a great modern critic. The whole business of 'influence' is much subtler than our crude use of the term allows. It is not a matter of 'agreement' with so-and-so; it is a matter of possession, after which 'agreement'—or disagreement—is redundant. Your sensibility has changed, while it is still your own. You borrow the vocabulary, the inflexions and gestures of another man, even, but they become yours, and filled with your identity. So in these splendid passages it is Jonson's voice we hear, and simultaneously that of the moral history of the language.

Early on he writes, 'A good life is a main argument' (p. 566);

it is in keeping that the metaphor for life comes from logic. A little later he proceeds:

> A man should so deliver himself to the nature of the subject whereof he speaks, that his hearer may take knowledge of his discipline with some delight: and so apparel fair and good matter that the studious of elegancy be not defrauded; redeem arts from their rough and braky seats . . . to a pure, open and flowery light, where they may take the eye and be taken by the hand.
>
> pp. 566–7

There follows the famous passage applauded by Eliot (and, improbably, Swinburne) in which Jonson rehearses Vivès's instruction to scrutinise but not worship the classics. 'Truth lies open to all; it is no man's several' (p. 567). A gift of the verse here bequeathed to the prose is the habit of concise and incisive generalisation. And then, a fine and embattled stance struck for independence:

> I am neither author, or fautor [patron] of any sect . . . if I have anything right, I defend it as truth's, not mine . . . it profits not me to have any man fence, or fight for me, to flourish, or take a side. Stand for truth, and 'tis enough.
>
> p. 568

It is the plainness, the forceful cadences which rescue this from platitude, and make it the writer's own. So, writing of acts of courtesy, he gives an aphorism roots in the tricks of his own London:

> he that doth them merely for his own sake is like one that feeds his cattle to sell them: he hath his horse well-dressed for Smithfield.
>
> p. 578

Horsemeat was just as nasty then as now.

The passages that count most describe the right style for speech, in verse or prose; but these passages mingle easily with those on moral behaviour, and at times (as they should be) the remarks which describe how to live well cannot be separated from how to write well. And even where there is a distinction, good writing never fails to be commensurate with values.

Others, . . . in composition are nothing, but what is rough and broken . . . They would not have it run without rubs, as if that style were strong and manly that struck the ear with a kind of unevenness. These men err not by chance, but knowingly, and willingly . . .

p. 585

Thus he admires one who 'never forced his language, nor went out of the highway of speaking' (p. 589), one (and he might be describing himself) whose 'language was . . . nobly censorious. No man ever spake more neatly, more pressly, more weightily, or suffered less emptiness, less idleness, in what he uttered. No member of his speech but consisted of the (*sic*) own graces' (p. 591). If we take this last, telling judgment and assimilate it to the following magnificent extract, we have a set of criteria against which to test Jonson and the finest English authors. Only masters pass.

The chief virtue of a style is perspicuity . . . A strict and succinct style is that where you can take away nothing without loss, and that loss to be manifest. The brief style is that which expresseth much in little . . . The congruent and harmonious fitting of parts in a sentence hath almost the fastening and force of knitting, and connection: as in stones well squared, which will rise strong a great way without mortar.

pp. 622–3

THE POEMS

As with Shakespeare's sonnets, it is hard to forbear quoting from *Timber*. I have held over one memorable pair of aphorisms to open discussion of the poems. He writes:

Language most shows a man: speak that I may see thee . . . No glass renders a man's form or likeness so true as his speech.

p. 625

I have spent some time describing the context of Jonson's work in order to recreate the remarkable force of the man and to suggest the points at which he felt his emotional and intellectual convictions as being at ease with the possibilities of the age. For his finest poems seem to me to be those which cherish and celebrate the most admirable parts of life, which make a statement about its richest sources, those which ensure continuity. Yet, as we have seen, Jonson was and is known for the harshness of his strictures upon contemporary life, for the blunt candour with which he spoke out against viciousness, malice and triviality, and in a few poems, for the traditional stoicism with which he put aside the claims of this world. In each case the language, as he asked, was true to the man, and the man was always amazingly true to his own sense of identity. The contradictions, as in all of us, were overcome as best he could; Jonson's finest poems meant that he reconciled the strong claims in him made by his classical traditions and by his immediate, vivid life in London. He brought to a full realisation a sense of history and a sense of the moment, and these issued in a statement to the future, in an offering made to posterity. And the statement is more than just a manifesto; it is the sum of a man's experience, deep, strong and engaged, which issues in the central parts of the work. Such an account would fit, I suppose, any great poet to whom we refer instinctively as a sure guide in charting our lives, but the example of Jonson is unusually pressing. He is himself so conscious of the poet's function, so determined that morality shall find its definitive utterance in poetry, and that the discovery, after strenuous exertion, shall come as a discovery of the right speech. It is this search and the consequent discoveries which concentrate his work. The job in hand is to find a kind of speech, a style in which to talk about ethical behaviour; it is the only honourable vocation for a man. Such a view of literature is as noble as it may be, and it belies as irrelevant the struggles of many subsequent poets to find subjects or forms. I do not wish to reduce the difficulties of being a poet, for they are many, but they may sometimes lie nearer home than some desperate endeavours suggest. Jonson saw the business as being explicitly moral and as so developing the powers of poetry that moral argument was sustained in the most deliberate and straightforward manner possible—a manner in which richness, subtlety and power proceed from the intelligence of the poet and not from the accidents of language or subject. Now there are poems of Jonson's which treat a specific and local subject, and I shall admire one of these in particular, *To Penshurst*. It may be objected that there he had a subject to hand—fine and rooted living—which later poets are denied. But as the poem reveals, Jonson uses Penshurst as the actual approximation to an ideal of civilisation, and moves surely from personal to impersonal tribute, from description to celebration. In so far as we are heirs to the great humanist ideas of the Renaissance—as I believe we are, though the ideas have passed through the transfiguration of romantic socialism—then what *To Penshurst* offers us is not regret for lost ways of life, but an example of how to value life. The poet should speak out against what he hates, as Jonson does, but above that his duty is to lives and ways of life which he may define and celebrate. Jonson lives for us because he relishes the duty. In speaking of this material Jonson is primarily making his own life, and making his life was to do with planning his work. We therefore return to the central issue which is to discover the unalterable way to say what must be said. This calls for a know-ledge of the history of literature and ideas, for experience of the actualities of one's time, for a solid grasp on the relationships between ideas and action, and between action and a style of writing; it calls for a command of technical detail, since slight technical details record the distinctions in moral perception. It therefore calls for genius. Hidden in *A Celebration of Charis (I)* are ten lines of Jonson's which render the task he saw for himself, and which in their beauty overcome it:

> Though I now write fifty years,
> I have had, and have my peers:
> Poets, though divine, are men;
> Some have loved as old again.
> And it is not always face,
> Clothes or fortune gives the grace,
> Or the feature, or the youth;
> But the language and the truth,
> With the ardour and the passion,
> Gives the lover weight and fashion.

I shall treat Jonson's poems in three groups: first, the slighter poems he wrote according to more conventional tastes than his own but for which he is well known and a few of which are as beautiful as any of his contemporaries'; second, poems, sometimes 'occasional', sometimes without formal prompting, which treat ethical or religious themes; third, poems arising from particular social contacts, with friends, patrons, fellow poets, or enemies. Obviously, all kinds of other groupings are feasible; one could work through the various volumes of the complete poems: *Epigrams, The Forest, The Underwood*, and the ungathered poems (a part of the complete poems was published with Jonson's preparation in 1616; the remainder three years after his death, in 1640). One could take the various forms one by one: epigrams, odes, songs, epistles and so on. Or one could just consider the best. In the groupings I propose there are a very few poems I would like to discard, and a few which are flawed; Jonson's greatest poems emerge about equally from his moral reflections and from his social life, and as they are great, they transcend a particular occasion, shake off the 'appropriate' manner, and speak of major matters in Jonson's major style. The poems are brief and various; the range of their experience is wide and their wisdom is profound and assured; Jonson omits the further reaches of experience and the vertiginous glimpses of the unknown we find in Shakespeare; if he neglects numinous mystery, none the less he holds on to values and reality with the peculiar patience of genius. His metaphysics (and they are there) are not those of Donne, the dazzling casuist, the lavish, incredibly rapid dialectician. Jonson's mind is 'mere English', working for clarity, for the empiricism of the English spirit, for a sceptical accuracy. The poems in which he achieves what he wants are also warm and human—no one could dilute Jonson's humanity. They are among the greatest poems in our literature.

Love Poems

The smaller love lyrics do as well as all that has gone before. One might suggest that Jonson took the native style as his point of departure for love poems in which to rival the Petrarchans, except that he has gone a long way beyond the bluntness of Gascoigne. He has learned the graces and the flexibilities of

Sidney, he can match Campion for mischief and sensuous delicacy. The famous 18th-century setting of *Drink to Me only with Thine Eyes* with its fat, lush melody, outrages all the poem's tact, its declared lightness of tone. Reading the poem, and forgetting (if we can) the tune, is to encounter an act of affectionate and ironically indulgent courtesy. Comparable virtues bring to life the famous love song *To Celia* from *Volpone*, inviting, in the manner of a score of others, of Marvell's *To His Coy Mistress* and Herrick's *To The Virgins*, the lady to oblige him while youth is on her side. As I have said in discussing Campion, these poems all derive from Catullus's *Vivamus, mea Lesbia, atque amemus*, and we may grasp (even without knowing Latin) how Jonson even more than his contemporaries was soaked in the ancient classics. This saturation, as *Timber* makes clear, means that the Latin issues not as stilted translation or as pedantry, but as a presence which informs the writing even when that writing is at its easiest and most idiomatic. Thus here the movement of the poem is unmistakably real and independent of sponsors; it is brisk and alert as it gives out the coolness of Jonson's persuasion:

> Come my Celia, let us prove
> While we may, the sports of love;
> Time will not be ours for ever,
> He, at length, our good will sever.
> Spend not then his gifts in vain.
> Suns that set may rise again,
> But if once we lose this light,
> 'Tis with us, perpetual night.

Comparable but gentle and less licentious is another song *To Celia* in octosyllabic couplets. The previous one is ostensibly Volpone's; snatches of the next appear in *Volpone*, but as a whole it is independent. Again, the light playfulness is fully authentic. This is not a poem 'about' flirtation; it is the act of flirtation magically realised and, in the tone, placed and valued.

> Kiss me sweet: the wary lover
> Can your favours keep, and cover,
> When the common courting jay
> All your bounties will betray.

Kiss again: no creature comes.
Kiss, and score up wealthy sums
On my lips . . .

Campion could not have bettered the amusement in Jonson's 'There you are!' when he wrote, 'Kiss again: . . .' He enforces the pause by the colon—then, 'no creature comes'. So, in abandonment and relief after the next 'kiss', the line soars right over the line-ending to 'lips' in the next. The refinement of this chaste style never falters, and any collection of Jonson's pieces in this vein would be ample enough to rival most poets whose reputation rests on their Courtly Love poetry alone. We do not find the passionate momentum of Shakespeare's sonnets in Jonson's love poetry, and this is partly because those subjects which pressed most heavily upon his creative powers did not emerge as love poetry. The stormy pleading of the sonnets strikes no answering note in Jonson's poetry.

The love poems do not confine themselves to mischief. The whole sequence *A Celebration of Charis* contains within its subtle couplets the quick, deft changes from disconsolation to delight and back. And in the fourth poem of the sequence, there occurs a stanza which is a touchstone for freshness and sharpness of imagery, speaking alike to Renaissance and Romantic criteria.

Have you seen but a bright lily grow,
    Before rude hands have touched it?
Have you marked but the fall o' the snow
    Before the soil hath smutched it?
Have you felt the wool of the beaver?
        Or swansdown ever?
Or have smelt the bud o' the briar?
        Or the nard in the fire?
    Or have tasted the bag of the bee?
O so white! O so soft! O so sweet is she!

The radiant images are allowed to do their work without emphasis, enhanced only by the light touch of 'bright', the contrast of 'smutched'; the sensuous delight gathers to an ecstasy in the breathless rhythms of the second half of the stanza. Yet this is not really characteristic Jonson. We do not, as we may even with such a minute stylist as George Herbert, think in Jonson's connection of original or daring imagery. Of course, there is a command of the musical resources of the language.

> Slow, slow, fresh fount, keep time with my salt tears;
> Yet slower, yet; O faintly, gentle springs;
> List to the heavy part the music bears,
> Woe weeps out her division when she sings.

The first line is utterly expert. The alliteration and the stresses are regularly struck yet so delayed and muted that they contribute only to the languour and loitering step of the line, and not at all to anything ponderous. The second line perfectly imitates the affected anguish of some fastidious conductor—'Yet slower, yet; O faintly, . . .'—as it also creates a tiny diversion in the plaintive melody. The song is a verbal equivalent of Dowland's wonderful *Lachrimae*. The varieties of speech-contour exactly suit the curve of feeling; Jonson's stanza-forms are as versatile as all the madrigalists'.

All the same, I think it is fair to say that in thinking of Jonson as an Elizabethan lyricist, we turn first to poems, sometimes from the masques, sometimes from elsewhere, of which *The Hymn to Diana* is representative:

> Queen and huntress, chaste and fair,
> Now the sun is laid to sleep,
> Seated in thy silver chair
> State in wonted manner keep:
>   Hesperus entreats thy light,
>   Goddess excellently bright.
>
> Lay thy bow of pearl apart,
> And thy crystal shining quiver;
> Give unto thy flying hart
> Space to breathe, how short soever,
>   Thou that mak'st a day of night,
>   Goddess excellently bright.

This ritual liturgy belongs to the intricate stylisation of the masques, and it derives from the conventions of pastoral Petrarchanism and from Arcadia. The restraint and stateliness of this is

Petrarchanism made public; Jonson catches exactly the hymnal simplicity needed for the procession which accompanies the queen. The profusion of Spenser is chastened; this language is at once silvered and ethereal and austerely controlled. Within the masque conventions, Jonson takes such writing with complete seriousness. His craftsmanship is impeccable. Yet it is not just Puritan to insist that in the end the convention is not serious, however professional the writer is about the writing. The chastity of the style is not won from writing this kind of thing, and however lovely it is, it is not as lovely as those poems of Campion's with more evident roots in the stuff of experience. These poems are part of Jonson's accomplishment, but he does not utter them from his depths.

One or two love poems come from the centre of the man. There is the famous *On My Picture Left in Scotland* which muses poignantly on his vanished physical charms and the failure of his verse to supplant the bright young Apollos. He glumly sees (though the total effect is more poised and deprecating than glum) that

> she cannot embrace,
> My Mountain belly and my rocky face...

Religious Poems

But in turning from the love poems to the second group I marked out, the group which deals with ethical or religious themes, we move in the best examples from delicately minor poetry to work of outright greatness. I shall begin with one of the best, the poem *To Heaven*:

> Good and great God, can I not think of Thee,
> But it must, straight, my melancholy be?
> Is it interpreted in me disease,
> That, laden with my sins, I seek for ease?
> 5   O, be thou witness, that the reins dost know
> And hearts of all, if I be sad for show;
> And judge me after, if I dare pretend
> To aught but grace, or aim at other end.
> As thou art all, so be thou all to me,

10　First, midst, and last, converted One and Three;
　　My faith, my hope, my love; and in this state,
　　My judge, my witness, and my advocate.
　　Where have I been this while exiled from thee?
　　And whither rapt, now thou but stoop'st to me?

15　Dwell, dwell here still! O being everywhere,
　　How can I doubt to find Thee ever here?
　　I know my state, both full of shame and scorn,
　　Conceived in sin, and unto labour born,
　　Standing with fear, and must with horror fall,

20　And destined unto judgement, after all.
　　I feel my griefs too, and there scarce is ground
　　Upon my flesh to inflict another wound.
　　Yet dare I not complain or wish for death
　　With holy Paul, lest it be thought the breath

25　Of discontent; or that these prayers be
　　For weariness of life, not love of thee.

　　(line 2. 'it must, straight, . . .' i.e. onlookers think this. l. 3. The
　　onlookers 'interpret in (him) disease . . .' l. 5. reins: seat of emotion
　　in Elizabethan physiology)

The style of this is plain and direct, as it is also sinewy and felici-
tous. The informing principle of the poem is expository, and
the one objection that may be brought against it is that the poem
starts out from a sense of personal affront. Jonson declares
himself wearied by those who always interpret his moments of
contemplation as moments of private melancholy. It is an appeal
to God for vindication and it thus involves a touch of pique
which taints the nobility of feeling. This fault apart, the styles
and the matter are firm. The couplet has never been better
handled; where Pope is most impressive there is likewise a
breathtaking facility which puts gravity like this out of reach.
Jonson's couplets are like 'stones well squared': they present a
polished and impressive surface—there is no break in the texture.
Yet the rhythmic control is never slack or in repose; he adjusts
the subdued variations to the precise expression of the feeling.
Thus in the first line the slight alliteration throws heavy, impressive weight on three of the first four syllables. Elsewhere the
placing of the caesura consolidates the meaning, as in the last

line where the essential opposition and paradox of the poem is held in balance, or as in lines 17–20 where the regular placing of the caesuras allows quiet but powerful feeling to accumulate in the repetition and to release itself in the long curve of line 20, halted in the finality, 'after all'. The triple units of lines 10–12 render the intellectual concept of the Trinity with exactitude and passion; the mystery of Three-in-One becomes immediate in the triple movements of single lines. A small device borrowed from the Petrarchans, such as 'everywhere'/'ever here' in 15–16, rises above a device, and becomes the only way to express the omnipresence of God. The poem states Jonson's own position with his habitual firmness: in line 17, 'I know', in line 21, 'I feel'; the movement of the couplets is assured, the argument confident, the tone crisp, and braced. But for all the steadiness of Jonson's stance, one cannot doubt its attendant grace and humility. The quickening of stresses in line 15, 'Dwell, dwell here still!' though logical ('where have I been . . .?') has the suddenness of rapturous terror. The moment is overcome, and the poet returns to the meditative statement of the behaviour open to him. Jonson faces the temptation of 'weariness of life' ('dare I not complain'), understands it, and puts it by; he overcomes gracelessness, and he wins, by command of the available arguments and checking them against experience, a stoic composure. Stoicism is not the only courage; it isn't even Jonson's only kind, but it is an honourable attitude, and here he gives it unforgettable expression. He transcends the exclusive truculence of Ralegh, the violence of feeling in some poems of Donne. *To Heaven* takes its place alongside the poems about death like Donne's *Hymn to God the Father* and George Herbert's *Church-Monuments* as living documents one can turn to endlessly; they uphold the high calling of the human mind.

These poems, and Jonson's with them, speak with the voice of the poet, and their power derives from his intelligence and his moral perception in an experience best understood by meeting it as straightforwardly as possible. Consequently, there is in such poems scarcely any imagery; the poem *is* its own image, and metaphor could do relatively little to help it. Control of diction and rhythm absorbs the poet. Another of Jonson's on a similar topic as *To Heaven* may, at the risk of repetition, illustrate the matter further. In *To the World: A Farewell for a Gentlewoman, Virtuous and Noble* Jonson gives his speech to a mature and disenchanted intelligence, commenting on the traps of her experience. Once more, the development is ordered by exposition; the metaphors are conventional, and the unifying principle is, apart from the argument, the attitude and tone of the speaker. The stanza form is one of the simplest in English: octosyllabic quatrains rhyming *abab*, yet the poem is in spite of the clarity not simple. The ease of manner, the mature acceptance of disillusion and death, rest upon a reality of felt experience which informs the poem. The cost exacted by life for maturity of attitude has been paid in full. The methods of Lord Vaux, Gascoigne, and Ralegh are now entire, replete with wisdom, subtle, sensitive, and definite. The last eight lines must suffice to demonstrate what the poem does. The language is typically lucid, the movement firm, the placing of the rhymes sure and relevant. The speaker knows where her identity lies and where her omissions, and she likewise turns, as we all do, back to the place where she belongs in order to meet the demands of time. There is no compromise, no stridency, no desperation.

> No, I do know that I was born
> To age, misfortune, sickness, grief;
> But I will bear these with that scorn
> As shall not need thy false relief.
> Nor for my peace will I go far,
> As wanderers do, that still do roam,
> But make my strengths, such as they are,
> Here in my bosom, and at home.

Other poems in this manner which deserve extremely close reading include *The Mind of the Frontispiece to a Book* (first printed in Ralegh's *The History of the World*), the *Hymn to God the Father*, the *Epode* 'Not to know vice at all . . .', and the faultless series of epitaphs. I shall close this brief examination of Jonson's religious poems by quoting the epitaph *On My First Son*, though the other, intolerably poignant epitaph *On My*

First Daughter is no less piercing, closing as it does with this couplet:

> This grave partakes the fleshly birth—
> Which cover lightly, gentle earth.

Perhaps this next epitaph is more moving simply because his son was seven years old when he died, and his daughter only six months.

> Farewell, thou child of my right hand, and joy;
> My sin was too much hope of thee, loved boy.
> Seven years thou wert lent to me, and I thee pay,
> Exacted by thy fate, on the just day.
> O, could I lose all father, now! For why
> Will man lament the state he should envy?
> To have so soon 'scaped world's and flesh's rage,
> And, if no other misery, yet age!
> Rest in soft peace; and, asked, say: Here doth lie
> Ben Jonson his best piece of poetry—
> For whose sake, henceforth, all his vows be such,
> As what he loves may never like too much.

Again, Jonson plays off the closed, trim form of the couplets against the rhythms of speech. This poem seeks more immediately than is usual with Jonson to reconcile a conflict—between the personal pain at the loss of his son, and the consolations of Christian doctrine: 'For why/Will man lament the state he should envy?' But man does, especially when he is a parent, and this poem records all the appropriate tenderness as well as the anguish. The poem is written in what *Timber* calls 'the concise style, which expresseth not enough, but leaves somewhat to be understood' (p. 623); the phrase 'yet age!' is left for the reader to fill in; the question 'why will man lament?' is left unanswered: the poem finds it answerable. At the end, he can only turn upon the pain and vow to avoid such pain again by so disciplining himself as not to admit such love. It is a grim resolve. The composure won by this poem is won by repression and severity, and it is worth proposing that the resignation of poems like *To the World* and *To Heaven* is complemented in Jonson by a titic generosity of spirit. He gave himself largely to the world, and was bruised so giving. The melancholy and the moroseness which he noted in himself (and parodied) came in those periods when he withdrew from the world in order to comprehend its cruelties. In the finest poems, the exuberance and the austerity come together and issue in the wise disillusion we have seen, or, more finely yet, in the unsentimental warmth and humane gratitude of active celebration. It is to poems of this kind that I now turn.

Social Poems

These poems arise from a variety of occasions. There are tributes paid to patrons, epistles to friends prompted by all kinds of causes some of which we have to guess at, and there are the writings specifically presented to 'The Tribe of Ben' which in one sense foreshadow the civil and sociable environment of the 18th-century coffee house, but which surpass the milieu of Dryden by a livelier as more profound justification for what they did. Jonson's poems for The Tribe, like (say) Carew's excellent reproach to the master beginning ' 'Tis true (dear Ben) . . .', carry within them not only social graces and ceremonies which are more than courtly, but also a grasp on the serious values, the sanctions without which the graces are frivolous games. Such attitudes made full and—if the word is not irretrievably disgraced— democratic contact possible. A man met another man openly, gladly.

The opening document for this sort of contact is the epistle *Inviting a Friend to Supper*. It does not involve the intimacy of other poems to The Tribe—that will come—but it sets the easy, courteous frame of reference within which intimacy is possible. The gregariousness of the friends was not possessive; it permitted the distance which, though not aloof, is necessary to individual delicacy of organisation. Jonson would have felt the force of Henry James's declaration that:

> I believe only in absolutely independent, individual and lonely virtue, and in the serenely unsociable (or if need be at a pinch sulky and sullen) practice of the same; the observation of a lifetime

> having convinced me that no fruit ripens but under that temporarily graceless rigour . . .

To John Bailey, 11 November 1912

The paradox is that Jonson, who is so often like his Augustan namesake Dr. Johnson, drew so much nourishment both from his solitude and his companionships. A tense balance of the two electrified his element. In the invitation, however, we see only the ease of company. Only by implication can we divine that such ease is the product of knowing how to speak to people without chumminess or reserve. The speech is hard to hit. Like all difficult art, you perfect it only by a combination of genius and civilisation. You begin here:

> Yet you shall have, to rectify your palate,
> An olive, capers, or some bitter salad
> Ushering the mutton; with a short-legged hen,
> If we can get her, full of eggs; and then
> Lemons, and wine for sauce . . .

The food is not everything; there is the talk:

> Howsoe'er, my man
> Shall read a piece of Virgil, Tacitus,
> Livy, or of some better book to us,
> Of which we'll speak our minds, amidst our meat;
> And I'll profess no verses to repeat . . .

And there is the drink—'which most doth take my muse and me . . . a pure cup of rich Canary wine'. But the evening will close, as it began, in comely moderation:

> Nor shall our cups make any guilty men,
> But at our parting, we will be as when
> We innocently met.

It is not merely Horation or hedonistic good-living Jonson is offering as a present; it is something tougher than a wine and food society. The something else is invoked in this next poem where in honouring a marriage and recovery from a dangerous wound (apparently after the bridegroom has won his wife from a rival by duelling), Jonson tenders moral advice to a headstrong

friend. He uses an ode-form but as we now expect transposes the
high style of an ode into a key more friendly and, here, direct:

> High-spirited friend,
> I send nor balms nor cor'sives to your wound,
>> Your fate hath found
> A gentler and more agile hand to tend
> The cure of that which is but corporal,
> And doubtful days (which were named critical)
>> Have made their fairest flight,
>> And now are out of sight.
> Yet doth some wholesome physic for the mind
>> Wrapped in this paper lie,
> Which in the taking if you misapply,
>>> You are unkind.
>
> Your covetous hand,
> Happy in that fair honour it hath gained,
>> Must now be reined.
> True valour doth her own renown command
> In one full action; nor have you now more
> To do, than be a husband of that store.
>> Think but how dear you bought
>> This same which you have caught,
> Such thoughts will make you more in love with truth.
>> 'Tis wisdom, and that high,
> For men to use their fortune reverently,
>>> Even in youth.

It is beautifully judged. The high rhetorical form is used to give
the syntax hesitation and delicacy. This is spoken straightly, but
with all the gentleness, affection and understanding in the world.
The reproachful close of each stanza prefigures Herbert both in
its judicious firmness and its mild cadence. The strong imperatives—'Must', 'Think'—check with the shifts of the form; the
respectful candour with which the large terms—'truth', 'wisdom',
'valour'—are offered precludes priggishness. The lady is never
directly spoken of, but in giving the advice Jonson manages at
the same time to exclude her from any blame, and pay her the
timely compliments concealed in 'gentler and more agile hand'
and the oblique (but not bashful) references in the second stanza.

It is a marvellous poem, and if today we cannot write one like it, then I suggest it is not because the movement of history (or whatever) has broken the concept of friendship, but simply because we do not try. And without civilising poems of this sort, we have no final standard by which to test our behaviour.

The many ideals latent in this poem abound in the epistles to his friends. Yet it misrepresents and abuses Jonson to speak as though one were hunting through his work for latent ideals. Each successful poem makes the ideals, the values and sanctions of an adult personality and a rich civilisation actual and vivid in a particular situation. It is one of Jonson's gifts to do this with a rare explicitness; the poems emerge from the life he led. He adopts no 'masks', no special *personae* worn for the poem, and then discarded. These procedures have their uses, but they shadow the poet in the poem. Jonson tries always to come at his utmost consistency and integrity of spirit in each one of his 'social' poems. He speaks from his full sense of himself to whoever it may be who listens. This means, given his imperfections, that he may be over-assertive or self-righteous in unseemly ways— the *Ode to Himself* is an example of this tendency. It means, as in several of the epigrams on Court figures, that he may be wantonly obscene or brutal, though sometimes the brutality may be called for, as in the savage epigram *On Sir Voluptuous Beast*, or that *On Gut*:

> *Gut* eats all day, and lechers all the night,
> So all his meat he tasteth over twice;
> And, striving so to double his delight,
> He makes himself a thoroughfare of vice.
> Thus in his belly can he change a sin,
> Lust it comes out, that gluttony went in.

A useful exercise in reading Elizabethan poetry would be to ponder the evidence of a training in logic, grammar, and rhetoric in this epigram. The finest 'social' poems, or poems of friendship, speak out with the same trenchancy in admiration of indispensable virtues. These poems not only recommend the virtues, they animate them; so that in reading the poem we experience the qualities. It is an active affair. So in the epigram to Camden (*14*), a little awkwardly perhaps, he pays tribute to Camden's exemplary union of classical and modern scholarship:

> Camden, most reverend head, to whom I owe
> All that I am in arts, all that I know . . .
> Pardon free truth, and let thy modesty
> Which conquers all, be once o'ercome by thee.
> Many of thine this better could, than I,
> But for their powers, accept my piety.

Jonson bore witness, as a matter of honour, to his masters; he paid his dues to his pieties—it is a lesson worth learning now when the factions of contemporary intellectuals plagiarise under cover of toadying. Each time, Jonson's epistles sound out bravely and directly. Thus to John Selden, acknowledging his book received,

> I know to whom I write. Here, I am sure,
> Though I am short, I cannot be obscure.

The long tribute to the patronage of Sir Edward Sackville strikes a slightly more deferential note, yet Jonson is still (as we would expect) brisk and manly. The lines carry themselves with an erect assurance, as of a man who knows his worth:

> You cannot doubt but I, who freely know
> This good from you, as freely will it owe;
> And though my fortune humble me, to take
> The smallest courtesies with thanks, I make
> Yet choice from whom I take them; and would shame
> To have such do me good, I durst not name;
> They are the noblest benefits, and sink
> Deepest in man, of which when he doth think,
> The memory delights him more from whom
> Than what he hath received. Gifts stink from some
> They are so long a-coming, and so hard;
> Where any deed is forced, the grace is marred.

The personal note and the impersonal chime together; once again, what in other hands would be platitudes, here quicken to the strength and unshakable integrity of the man who speaks them. And so it is that we know from the art—in its organised and self-conscious fullness—what we would have admired in Jonson the man, had we known him. One could multiply the evidence. There is the striking *Epitaph to Master Vincent Corbet* in which lightness and gravity of touch justly combine in order to give us the subject, Corbet, and Jonson's valuation of him at the same time. There is the well-known, little-read and generous memorial to Shakespeare ('To draw no envy (Shakespeare) on thy name'). There is the handsome brevity of another poem to a patron, the epigram (76) on *Lucy, Countess of Bedford*, which demands quotation, though the poem is densely woven and selection must mutilate it. He describes his ideal patroness, and in a polished turn at the last couplet finds that the Countess fits his model:

> I meant she should be courteous, facile, sweet,
> Hating that solemn vice of greatness, pride;
> I meant each softest virtue there should meet,
> Fit in that softer bosom to reside.
>
> Only a learned and a manly soul
> I purposed her; that should, with even powers,
> The rock, the spindle, and the shears control
> Of destiny, and spin her own free hours.

It would be pedantic to say these things again were it not that Jonson's greatness has been sold so short. Once more, in the absence of developed metaphors, it is the mastery of tone and rhythmic control which resolves the poem. The style is entire, powerful and sensitive. The repetitions of 'I meant' make it clear that Jonson wishes to set his own mark on the poem, but he judges his own place in it. And while the terms of approbation are completely his own, especially in these trenchant lines—

> I meant to make her fair and free and wise,
> Of greatest blood, and yet more good than great—

his eye remains steadily upon the subject and does not turn aside either into little ceremonies or into decoration. The relevance, the intellectual closeness of the poem form his compliment. To be fully intelligent is to make his bow.

The last two poems I wish to discuss in this (roughly speaking) social group are the famous address *To Penshurst*, family seat of Sidney's brother and a centre of civilised discussion and thought, and the *Elegy* beginning 'Though beauty be the mark of praise'. *To Penshurst* is 102 lines in length, it is closely modelled upon a Latin poem by Martial, and Jonson as in most of the celebratory epistles writes in couplets. The poem represents one of the peaks of Renaissance civilisation: the author, a product of the finest kinds of classical and Elizabethan training, himself a sturdily original temperament as well as a mighty intelligence, pays homage to a kind of living which embodies the richest potentialities of human contact and co-operation. Necessarily, the art of living in *To Penshurst* is not 'democratic' as we would know it. But the poem cannot be treated in class terms at all. We are ourselves too quick to call conscientiously anxious clichés to mind when the word 'class' crops up; this poem realises for us the mutual ceremonies and sanctions of a coherent way of life, and if no local pattern of living could be the same today, yet the values implicit in what Jonson's steadfast affection and straightness of judgment make alive to us are still alive and recognisable in their different forms. I certainly have no wish to resurrect the kind of aristocratic hauteur and reckless riding to hounds of which W. B. Yeats so much regretted the loss. But Jonson's poem gives us—as a matter of felt life—a more robust, less socially specific code of behaviour, though the poem handles the stuff of a housewife's life with engaging familiarity. We move (in feeling and in action) with the firm cadences of Jonson's voice and attitudes as he speaks to the life he enjoys. We participate in a sort of ritual, a festivity; we pay our homage, with wit, gentleness, and dignity to forms of human decency and kindness. Why should we not write like this today?

> And if the high-swol'n Medway fail thy dish,
> Thou hast thy ponds, that pay thee tribute fish,
> Fat, aged carps, that run into thy net.
> And pikes, now weary their own kind to eat,
> As loth the second draught or cast to stay,
> Officiously, at first themselves betray.

Bright eels that emulate them, and leap on land,
Before the fisher, or into his hand.
Then hath thy orchard fruit, thy garden flowers,
Fresh as the art and new as are the hours.
The early cherry, with the later plum,
Fig, grape and quince, each in his time does come:
The blushing apricot and woolly peach
Hang on thy walls that every child may reach.

It is a grand vision, gently hyperbolic (about the fish) but rich with a sense of cultivated and deliberate plenty. The landscape is not only fertile, it is serene and ordered by human reason, human providence and affection. There is no brutality—

And though thy walls be of the country stone,
They're reared with no man's ruin, no man's groan,
There's none that dwells about them, wish them down;
But all come in, the farmer and the clown . . .

One attractive and reliable measure of Jonson's gift as a poet is the way in which here, as in *Inviting a Friend to Supper*, as, indeed, in *Volpone* or *The Alchemist*, he can use tasty, juicy food to express moral realities. Here the food is all goodness and giving. The poem fills with a sense of place, of wholesome and rooted living in a way of life which takes in farming, sport, marriage, and family love. Such a sense, as we find it here, in places in Pope, in Wordsworth, George Eliot, and Lawrence, is a keen and abiding mark of the Englishness of English literature. It is worth noting that Wordsworth knew *To Penshurst* by heart; I think it among the greatest of Nature poems, for its terms of reference take in so much more than the individual. The last two couplets, in their beautiful seriousness and irresistible precision of judgments—the old, censorious Jonson flashes out—come to rest upon a verb. The present indicative 'dwells' summarises the argument, and extends the poem onwards into time. It is fair to call such a faith in continuity, religious.

Now, Penshurst, they that will proportion thee
With other edifices, when they see
Those proud, ambitious heaps, and nothing else,
May say, their lords have built, but thy lord dwells.

The last poem, though smaller in scope, is flawless. The odd line in *To Penshurst* lumbers a little; the *Elegy* is brief, succinct and springy. It takes what it needs from the song tradition, and what it needs from Jonson's own grave cast of mind, and his training in classical economy and the native style. A study of this poem should illuminate all I have proposed about the making of English poetry.

> Though beauty be the mark of praise,
> And yours of whom I sing be such
> As not the world can praise too much,
> Yet is't your virtue now I raise.
>
> A virtue like alloy, so gone
> Throughout your form, as though that move,
> And draw, and conquer all men's love,
> This subjects you to love of one,
>
> Wherein you triumph yet; because
> 'Tis of your self, and that you use
> The noblest freedom, not to choose
> Against or faith, or honour's laws.
>
> But who should less expect from you,
> In whom alone love lives again?
> By whom he is restored to men,
> And kept, and bred, and brought up true.
>
> His falling temples you have reared,
> The withered garlands ta'en away;
> His altars kept from the decay
> That envy wished and nature feared.
>
> And on them burn so chaste a flame
> With so much loyalty's expense,
> As Love, to acquit such excellence,
> Is gone himself into your name.
>
> And you are he: the deity
> To whom all lovers are designed,
> That would their better objects find:
> Among which faithful troop am I.

Who as an offering at your shrine,
Have sung this hymn, and here entreat
One spark of your diviner heat
To light upon a love of mine.

Which if it kindle not, but scant
Appear, and that to shortest view,
Yet give me leave to adore in you
What I, in her, am grieved to want.

The poem praises a friend, but explicitly sets aside the courtly convention; it is a poem about friendship, not about love, and it therefore avoids the temptations of mannerism and cliché. Yet he praises the friend's capacity to love and therefore can appropriately borrow the Petrarchan metaphors, especially the metaphorical deification, without sounding absurd. He honours the friend for her integrity in love at a time when love is become disreputable, and this integrity he catches and holds in the fragile, haunting rhythms of the fifth stanza. He perfectly justifies the stylised wardrobe by the fragile step of the movement, at delicate contrast with the stronger gallantry of the third stanza. But there is more than gallantry here: there is the power and fullness of a poet in absolute command of his theme. There is the richness and extraordinary subtlety of organisation available only to a poet of refinement as well as genius. There is the unimpeded voice of a great intelligence speaking on a serious subject with all the skill at his disposal. The language is naked, the argument true, the development impeccable, and the poem should move all of us, in so far as we are human beings and not sentimentalists, and move us in heart and mind alike. Such poetry nurtures and cherishes the human spirit, and gives it significance to live by; it fulfils a moral and literary tradition. It abides the intervening centuries, and it holds up now. The style and the man are one.

8

The Making of English Poetry

The principle of selection in this volume is a very exclusive one and it may be damagingly objected that where so many poets have been set aside or scantly treated one cannot claim to describe the influence of one writer on another or the establishment of one way of writing. Yet the concepts of 'influence' and 'tradition' are obscure and often nebulous, and it is rarely a useful business to guess at their origins in historical terms. We might say, for example, that Sidney 'influenced' George Herbert because there are moments when one reminds us of the other. We trace an ideal line of development from Wyatt through Sidney and Shakespeare to Donne and Marvell, and in so doing assimilate poem to poem and subject to subject and conclude that these poems and poets constitute the historical, unalterable order of Elizabethan poetry. But the affinity of poems is subtler than this definite procedure allows. An adequate literary history cannot afford to extrapolate only what it is interested in. It must attempt to settle the available evidence within as rich a descriptive context as possible. Only then will the complex and contradictory relations between poems and poet receive justice. I have already tried to issue a warning against the dangers of historical classification—of calling a poem 'Donneish' or 'Metaphysical' and saying no more than that it possesses the characteristics so labelled. To some extent one needs the labels; I have made considerable play with the term 'Petrarchan' in these pages. But the point is that we should attempt to recognise the variousness both of an historical period and of its personalities, and not attempt to blunt the variousness by roughness of classification. The Elizabethan period contains a tremendous amount of bad poetry, and a welter of conflicting intellectual, moral and economic conditions. My first chapter intends no more than the most provisional charting of the main presences. After looking one by one at the line of poets I offer, however, it is timely to return them to the texture of Elizabethan life. There are two problems that we need to study. The first is to attempt a description of how, if at all, one may use the concepts 'tradition' and 'influence', and thence to describe what this book sets out to do. The second problem is more acutely personal: it is a matter of deciding upon the value of reading the poems I have chosen. If they are woven so tightly into the stuff of a different historical context, how do we decide whether they are any good, or are we for ever insulated from the poems by our differences? When, as now, we are sunk in moral contradiction and conceptual conflict, how do we sort amongst poems of another age without becoming hopelessly lost in idiosyncrasy? It is the central difficulty of criticism and study of literature, but it will be worth rehearsing the arguments after attending to some poetry which has (I believe) been in many cases neglected or misunderstood.

First then, the use of 'influence' and 'tradition'. This account of the great Elizabethans closes with Ben Jonson; it is in him that the conflicting developments of the growing national poetry triumphantly reconcile themselves. But as is clear from his rewritings of Vivès in *Timber* and his use of Martial in *To Penshurst*, Jonson was not simply 'influenced' by these writers. They had, as we say, become a part of him. They moved inextricably in his mind; they altered his life; he possessed them. The absorption, the saturation in the material which I am trying to describe, is given us memorably here in this poem by Wallace Stevens:

The house was quiet and the world was calm.
The reader became the book; and summer night

Was like the conscious being of the book.
The house was quiet and the world was calm.

The words were spoken as if there was no book,
Except that the reader leaned above the page,

Wanted to lean, wanted much most to be
The scholar to whom his book is true, to whom

The summer night is like a perfection of thought.
The house was quiet because it had to be.

The quiet was part of the meaning, part of the mind:
The access of perfection to the page.

And the world was calm. The truth in a calm world,
In which there is no other meaning, itself

Is calm, itself is summer and night, itself
Is the reader leaning late and reading there.

It is a perfect poem. It describes an experience known to everyone who takes his reading seriously. In the quiet of late reading, the rhythms of the book and the unbroken response of the attentive reader move together as one activity, and the statement of the book is unfaltering. At the end of such reading, you lay down the book and, bound still by the spell of the experience, the statement settles into its place and becomes steady. You see it for what it is. History is become Now. The feeling of the poem and of the centuries pours into your mind and, before draining into your personality, fills it. It is in this process, lengthily sustained, that you shape your life and draw together your personality as best you can. Stevens communicates an action known to Ben Jonson and to himself, and he achieves all he does in a diction and movement so spare as to be almost unnoticeable, and in so doing Stevens has drawn upon the ease, the imperturbable urbanity which became possible at the intervention of Ben Jonson. This is not to say that Stevens drew directly on Jonson to write this poem. What happens is instead what the poem describes. In the course of his reading, the poet turns repeatedly to those writers who are his enduring references. They help to construct his temperament as they shape his speech. The temperament and the speech are still the poet's own, just as the reading has become the poet's own. The past is present in him.

It is in something like this provisional, allusive way that we may talk of 'influence'. The 'influences' operate within a total historical context, and it is anomalous in any attempt at a literary history to isolate only the major figures. In such a history, the concept 'tradition' signifies a body of learning and a way of writing, the two mixing and reacting so that one is uncertain as to which is sponsor in a given poem. The tradition of the plain style amongst the Elizabethans signifies the procedures of poetry certain men learned and practised; it signifies the potential poems within a body of collective experience, the experience being organised and marked out according to given rules and structures of poetry. The plain style, like any other style, observed certain principles of order, and these adapted themselves to the changes demanded by new principles—those which came from music, for example, and those which came from Italy. Every poem constitutes a redefinition of the tradition according to its changing and persistent principles. Wyatt, Ralegh, Campion, Jonson, each takes the old principles of the tradition, the rules, structures and procedures, and gives them in each poem a new specification. But their specifications, their poems are of a different order to those in which other poets of the same traditions make *their* specifications. They are different because they are better. The principles are called in their case to the service of greater resources and to define greater experience and subjects. It is at this point that we move from my first to my second problem, from trying to understand how to use the words 'influence' and 'tradition' properly to drawing up a list of the poems that matter most to us. For the great poems of the Elizabethan period, which I have reviewed in the foregoing chapters, come together by virtue of their greatness. As Yvor Winters says, 'it is my own conviction that one cannot write the history of poetry unless one can find the best poems. The best poems are the essential facts from which the historian must proceed.' This volume is not offered as a history; I try to select the best poems. Now the best poems have a good deal in common, and as they come together in their greatness and their comparability, it seems arguable that they realise certain qualities and principles which recur throughout the best English poetry which follows. Let me list a small group of poems, and let the reader compare them: Wyatt's *If Thou Wilt Mighty Be*, Gascoigne's *Woodman-ship* in its closing lines, Ralegh's *Even Such is Time*, Greville's *Caelica 69*, Shakespeare's *Sonnet 73*, Jonson's *To The World, A Farewell*, and add to these Donne's *Hymn to God the Father*, Herbert's *The Flower*. These poems are original in that the voice which utters them is rare, pure and intelligent. There are few innovations. There is little elaboration of imagery or drama of language. The poet speaks out plainly, and declares his intelligence, his power of feeling and the pressure of his living experience. These things live in the hard density of the language and its movement, and one finds, if one is diligent and delicate of study, that within the lineaments of the great Elizabethan poems there is a steadiness and a distinct integrity. It is the integrity of English poetry, for these poems are the making of English poetry and its Englishness. The ideal centre of a language lies in the configuration of its greatest poems, as another essential part of a nation's life lies amongst the continuity of its noblest buildings or its music. Indeed, the sturdiness of its morality rests in the endurance of these poems or ways of building, so that if the qualities made actual in English poetry were to lapse, then some vital centre of our moral living would crumble away, and our identity start to disintegrate. To say that is not to be guilty either of irrelevant patriotism or of false claims to absolute ideals in poetry and values. A concern with national identity is in place, because until we know what our own language can say we do not know who we are, and in that ignorance know nobody else either. It is no less important to grasp that in speaking as I do of a persistent set of characteristic qualities and styles of writing (which I find admirable) I am not claiming the absolute truth of what each poet says. We live, after all, with the inheritance of a number of both interwoven and incongruent moral and literary vocabularies. I have suggested many times that Renaissance Humanism set a mark within our personalities which is still visible, but since then a variety of contradicting ethics have struck sharply upon our moral sense. Romanticism, Scientific Rationalism, Marxist Democracy, Utilitarianism have introduced their prescriptions into our vocabulary. The literary alterations of principle have gone with them. But to recognise the conflict does not mean that we are condemned to individualist chaos within which every man's judgment is right for himself. We might do better to look at the forms of life and the views of human nature (and the two go together) which seem to form some kind of unity across the centuries. We then incorporate these into the moral and literary principles which we bring to bear upon today. The literature is not just a matter of providing principles, but of offering a principled experience for us to live through. The poetry of the past provides us with a vocabulary within which we may make our moral choices. The poets working between about 1540 and 1630 constructed the major principles and procedures of English poetry; they sent the language on its way fully formed. The great poets since then extended what those men did, they read and reread what had been done and they pushed forward, but any changes they wrought built upon the work already made. The style and the matter was firm and undated: it would accommodate what the later men had to say.

I shall close by describing what seems to me the essential line of the short poem in English. These are by the poets who have kept alive the shaping spirit, and born witness to the continuity of the race. They are mostly famous names, but the treatment proposed in this book and the addition of one or two extra names may suggest the identity and continuity which I urge upon the reader and wish to affirm and honour. After the men I have named and including Donne and George Herbert, I would group together Carew, a few poems by Herrick, Henry Vaughan (in, say, *To His Books* or *The Timber*), Andrew Marvell (who follows so much the spirit of Jonson), Pope (in *The Moral Essays*), Dr. Johnson (everywhere in his non-dramatic verse a powerful, deliberate poet,) Charles Churchill, George Crabbe, Wordsworth (who constantly refers to Jonson in the *Letters*) especially in *The Excursion* and *Michael*, Thomas Hardy (especially in *After a Journey* or *Neutral Tones*), Edward Thomas, Isaac Rosenberg; and then one casts uncertainly about. It is probably not useful here to guess at the upholders of the tradition writing since 1920. The enterprise is too hefty to skimp. But the list I offer embodies in the right poems the great strengths, the tact and resilience of the spirit of English poetry. Each of these men animated the traditional metres to do his work. Each speaks in his own voice, emphatic, direct, close. Their utterance is as intelligent as they can make it. They tend to avoid dramatic immediacy and contemporary fashion; they wear no masks. They speak out against what they hate, and they cherish and celebrate the best kinds of human contact. They are, to put it crudely, on the side of life. Their unmannered, scrupulous attention to humanity and the human future makes such writing as important now as it always was. The great Elizabethans stand at the head of a line pointing the way to intelligent resolution and faith in the present, and the present as leading into the future. We cannot, for all the differences, do without what they have to offer. They sustain strength and fineness.

Bibliography

The formative and most vigorously prompting essays upon poets I have discussed are Yvor Winters' three remarkable contributions to *Poetry* (Chicago) in February, March, and April 1939, and his penetrating and original observations upon Shakespeare's sonnets in an essay contributed to *Four Poets on Poetry*, ed. Don Cameron Allen (Johns Hopkins Press, Baltimore, 1959). (All these essays have become available since I finished this book in Winters' last collection *Forms of Discovery* (Alan Swallow, Denver, Colorado); he has, however, revised them and to my mind slightly damaged them). Although much of these essays by Winters is simply a matter of quotation and list, the bare, essential argument is highly original and compelling. I am here walking in that fine man's snow.

Apart from this general and omnipresent indebtedness, I shall cite those essays and books which I found useful according to the chapters where they are relevant. There is an enormous bulk of commentary on the Elizabethans, and much I haven't read and much, though heavy with the machinery of the New and the Old Bibliography, is immensely boring. I should mention, however, two general studies which the reader who intends to explore this ground thoroughly may care to look up. The first, which I could not use because it is only just published, follows also and in more specialist detail in Yvor Winters' footsteps; it is called *The English Lyric from Wyatt to Donne: A History of the Plain and Eloquent Styles*, by Douglas L. Peterson (Princeton 1967). The second, which I have read two or three times, is Rosamond Tuve's bulky, wayward, confusing, and intermittently invaluable study *Elizabethan and Metaphysical Imagery* (Chicago 1947) and which protests the most headlong claims I know for the historicist approach.

Finally, I also cite the editions which I have used (and modernised for myself) chapter by chapter. But as I have mentioned in my preface, I make extensive use of John Williams's very ample anthology of the relevant work, *English Renaissance Poetry* (Doubleday 1963); I hope also that it is not immodest to point towards my own anthology *English Poetry 1550-1660* (Methuen 1965) as providing many of the texts I discuss and as offering at least a partial embodiment of the great Elizabethans.

CHAPTER 1: THE ELIZABETHAN MOMENT

H. Craig: *The Enchanted Glass: The Elizabethan Mind in Literature* (Oxford 1936).

W. Haller: *The Rise of Puritanism* (Columbia 1938).

L. Stone: *The Crisis of the Aristocracy 1558–1641* (Oxford 1965).

Trevor Aston ed.: *Crisis in Europe 1560–1660* (esp. papers by E. J. Hobsbawm and H. R. Trevor-Roper) (Routledge 1965).

R. R. Bolgar: *The Classical Heritage and its Beneficiaries* (Cambridge 1963, pp. 239–317).

H. A. Mason: *Humanism and Poetry in the Early Tudor Period* (Routledge 1959).

John Stevens: *Music and Poetry in the Tudor Court* (Cambridge 1962).

W. Mellers: *Music and Society* (Dobson 1950, esp. chaps. 2–5).

M. Girouard: *Robert Smythson and the Architecture of the Elizabethan Era* (Country Life 1966).

(The figures about national incomes in Elizabethan times I owe to Alan Everitt's paper 'Social Mobility in England 1500–1700', *Past and Present* 33, April 1966.)

CHAPTER 2: WYATT

H. A. Mason: already cited.

J. V. Cunningham: *Tradition and Poetic Structure* (Swallow 1960, pp. 40–59).

Wyatt: *Collected Poems*, ed. K. Muir (Muses Library, Routledge 1949).

CHAPTER 3: VAUX, GASCOIGNE, NASHE, RALEGH

J. V. Cunningham: already cited.

Alan Stephens: *Selected Poems of Barnabe Googe* (Swallow 1961, introduction).

D. A. Davie: 'A Reading of Ocean's Love to Cynthia' in *Stratford on Avon Studies 2, Elizabethan Poetry*, ed. J. R. Brown and B. Harris (Arnold 1961).

Ralegh: *The Poems*, ed. Latham (Muses Library, Routledge 1951).

CHAPTER 4: SPENSER, SIDNEY AND SOUTHWELL

John Buxton: *Sir Philip Sidney and the English Renaissance* (rev. edition, Macmillan 1964).

J. C. A. Rathmell: *The Psalms of Sir Philip Sidney and the Countess of Pembroke* (Doubleday 1963, pp. xi–xxxviii, and text).

Sidney: *The Poems*, ed. W. A. Ringler (Oxford 1962).

Louis Martz: *The Poetry of Meditation* (Yale 1954, passim).

CHAPTER 5: THE MADRIGALISTS AND CAMPION

W. Mellers: already cited

Gustave Reese: *Music in the Renaissance* (Dent 1947).

B. Pattison: *Music and Poetry of the English Renaissance* (Methuen 1948).

Auden, Kallman, Greenberg ed.: *An Elizabethan Song Book* (Faber 1957).

E. H. Fellowes ed.: *English Madrigal Verse*, 3rd edition revised and enlarged by F. W. Sternfeld and D. Grear (Oxford 1967).

D. Stevens ed.: *The Penguin Book of English Madrigals* (Penguin 1967).

Campion: *Works*, ed. Vivian (Oxford 1909).

CHAPTER 6: GREVILLE AND SHAKESPEARE'S SONNETS

James Smith: 'On Metaphysical Poetry', *Scrutiny II*, pp. 222–39.

B. Herrnstein ed.: *Discussions of Shakespeare's Sonnets* (Heath, Boston 1964).

L. C. Knights: 'Shakespeare's Sonnets' in *Explorations* (Chatto 1946).

D. A. Traversi: 'The Sonnets' in *An Approach to Shakespeare* (Doubleday 1956).

W. Empson: *Seven Types of Ambiguity* (Chatto 1930, passim).

J. W. Lever: *The Elizabethan Love Sonnet* (Methuen 1956, pp. 162–273).

J. B. Leishman: *Themes and Variations in Shakespeare's Sonnets* (Oxford 1961).

Greville: *Works Vol. 2. (Caelica)* ed. Bullough (Oliver and Boyd, 1945). *Selected Poems*, ed. Thom Gunn (Faber 1968).

Shakespeare: *Sonnets*, ed. C. Knox-Pooler (Arden edition, Methuen 1931).

CHAPTER 7: JONSON

Geoffrey Walton: *Metaphysical to Augustan: Studies in Tone and Sensibility in the 17th Century* (Bowes and Bowes 1955, pp. 23–44).

F. R. Leavis: 'The Line of Wit' in *Revaluation* (Chatto 1936).

Jonson: *The Poems and Prose Works*, ed. C. H. Herford and P. and E. Simpson (Oxford 1947).

CHAPTER 8

The argument of this chapter is, I believe, new; but I owe more than I can say to discussion with Mr. Quentin Skinner and to his daring and brilliant paper 'The Limits of Historical Explanation', *Philosophy*, July 1966.

RECORDS

Instrumental Music from the Courts of Queen Elizabeth and King James Brunswick (Decca) AXTL 1099

Music of the High Renaissance in England Turnabout (Vox) TV 4017

Tallis: Tudor Church Music 1 and 2 Argo RG 436/479

William Byrd: Mass for Five Voices Argo RG 226

Tavern Songs, Catches, Glees and Other Diverse Entertainments of Merrie England Vanguard BG 561

Madrigal Masterpieces Vanguard BG 604

Orlando Gibbons: Tudor Church Music Argo RG 80

Elizabethan and Restoration Vocal Music Saga XLD 5222

Julian Bream Plays Dowland Westminster XWN 18429

The Royal Brass Music of James I L'Oiseau-Lyre OL 50189

Shakespeare Songs and Lute Solos HMV Alp 1265

John Dowland: The First Book of Ayres Dover HLR 5220

'Sing we at Pleasure' HMV HQM/S 1080

Index

Main entries are indicated by heavy type